Quarterly Essay

CONTENTS

Quarterly Essay is published four times a year by Black Inc., an imprint of Schwartz Media Pty Ltd. Publisher: Morry Schwartz.

ISBN 978-1-86395-457-0 ISSN 1832-0953

Subscriptions – 1 year (4 issues): $49 within Australia incl. GST. Outside Australia $79.
2 years (8 issues): $95 within Australia incl. GST. Outside Australia $155.
Payment may be made by Mastercard or Visa, or by cheque made out to Schwartz Media. Payment includes postage and handling.

To subscribe, fill out and post the subscription card, or subscribe online at:

www.quarterlyessay.com

Correspondence and subscriptions should be addressed to the Editor at:

Black Inc. Level 5, 289 Flinders Lane Melbourne VIC 3000 Australia
Phone: 61 3 9654 2000 / Fax: 61 3 9654 2290
Email:
quarterlyessay@blackincbooks.com (editorial)
subscribe@blackincbooks.com (subscriptions)

Editor: Chris Feik. Management: Sophy Williams, Caitlin Yates. Publicity: Elisabeth Young. Design: Guy Mirabella. Production Co-ordinator: Adam Shaw

AUSTRALIAN STORY

Kevin Rudd and the Lucky Country

Mungo MacCallum

This is the nightmare.

You are naked and lost and in desperate need of help. Around you the countryside is familiar, but all the usual landmarks have vanished, along with the roads and tracks. Signposts have been obliterated. You look in vain for a way out, and realise that there is nowhere safe to go. Storms are approaching from all sides, the ground is heaving as if in an earthquake and the horizon rears up as a tsunami gathers.

All seems lost, and then you feel a reassuring tap on the shoulder. You turn to see a funny little man, who says: "Hello. My name is Kevin, I'm from Queensland and I'm here to help." With a scream of despair you wake, and then you go on screaming because it was all true. It is 16 September 2008: Lehman Brothers has collapsed, signalling the end of the world as we knew it. Just as socialism was seen to have failed with the unravelling of the Soviet Union in the 1990s, the basis of the capitalist system must now be called into question. The global financial markets can no longer be trusted, and all ahead is gloom, doom and above all uncertainty.

It is a situation that calls for superlative leadership: the iron resolve of John Curtin, the imperturbable authority of Robert Menzies, the towering intellect of Gough Whitlam, the comforting charisma of Bob Hawke, the flair and daring of Paul Keating, the dogged reliability of John Howard. Instead we are stuck with an untried, God-bothering shiny-bum whose idea of a crisis is a joke that fell flat on commercial television.

But here is the tag line: not only do we accept him, we welcome him with adulation. Suddenly the nerd from Nambour is our trusted saviour. It is, to put it mildly, an unlikely apotheosis, but then Kevin Michael Rudd is in many ways an unlikely politician. While he spent a long time working for a Labor premier, Queensland's Wayne Goss, he was never a Labor apparatchik; he did not fight his way up through the ranks in the manner of a Paul Keating or a Mark Latham. He lacks their visceral hatred for their political opponents, but equally he often appears to lack their unquestioning commitment to the Labor cause. On the surface, at least, Rudd might appear comfortable sitting on the conservative benches in parliament; he has much in common with Liberal moderates, such as Petro Georgiou and Judi Moylan, and of course he had a personal friendship with Joe Hockey, now himself a potential aspirant to the Lodge – although that may have lapsed in the recent heat of battle.

Unusually, he is open about his Christian beliefs, which has led Janet Albrechtsen, in an outburst of bile notable even for the Murdoch press's resident dominatrix, to snarl: "Our man in the Lodge is so full of hubris that he uses his religious beliefs for some particularly base political purposes." But he is generally less forthcoming about his political convictions, so much so that one critic, Greg Melleuish, has described him as "Australia's first postmodern prime minister." By this Melleuish did not mean that Rudd was a student of semiotics, but that he lacked any firmly held principles or beliefs.

It is a charge which others on the Right have made before: they concede, reluctantly, that Rudd is a brilliant political operator, but then jump to the conclusion that he is all spin and no substance. This judgment is based almost entirely on a single fact: Rudd, before the 2007 election, declared himself to be an "economic conservative." But in dealing with the global financial meltdown he has proved to be a born-again Keynesian, willing to embrace both deficit and debt as the price of economic stimulus.

This is seen as a contradiction, but is it really? Rudd never claimed to be an economic neo-liberal, dedicated to a balanced budget at all times, irrespective of the circumstances. What he did promise was to keep a balance over the course of the economic cycle, surely a conservative approach. This obviously meant delivering surpluses over the boom years, but it did not preclude going into deficit when the busts came. And given that the bust of 2008 was the biggest for at least eighty years, his spending program was hardly an unorthodox response. And he promised to return the budget to surplus as soon as possible after the recovery came. The truly radical approach would have been to cut spending to match the loss of revenue, which is what the more wild-eyed of the neo-liberals in America were demanding. This was the so-called "conservative" solution, which failed so spectacularly during the Great Depression. Not even the most hide-bound Tory would want to repeat that experience.

Rudd has further confused people by describing himself, admittedly some time ago, as a Christian socialist. Given that in Australia socialist has come to mean left-winger, practically communist, some of the commentariat appear to believe that behind the mild-mannered façade lurks a rabid Trotskyite ready to emerge when the time is right. But if Rudd is to be judged by his actions rather than by the fantasies of the Right, he comes through as a pretty straightforward social democrat, accepting the broad tenets of capitalism provided that it can be regulated in ways necessary to make it a tool of a civilised and compassionate society. Hardly revolutionary, but perhaps not ideological enough to satisfy the pundits who seek to attach precise labels to their politicians.

The confusion over Rudd has a long history among the commentariat, dating back to the time he assumed the Labor leadership, and even before that. When Rudd sought to explain himself in two essays in the *Monthly* concerning the way his Christian beliefs informed his Labor politics and rejecting the Coalition's attempts to claim a religious monopoly, it was widely seen within the Canberra press gallery as a purely political manoeuvre, an attempt to draw attention to his leadership credentials. And when his approval ratings rose to stratospheric heights and remained there, the assumption was that the general public simply didn't know or understand him; they were dazzled by his novelty, but sooner or later they would wake up to the fact that he was just another clever politician.

But perhaps, just perhaps, the voters saw Rudd more clearly than the insiders, and they liked what they saw. Early in 2009 a letter writer to the *Sydney Morning Herald* summed it up in one word: integrity. Far from being the Machiavellian manipulator the commentators portrayed, Rudd was both principled and honest. And it was these attributes that the punters trusted as he began to tackle the global financial crisis, an unexpected catastrophe not of his making.

Many of Australia's twenty-six prime ministers have faced similar challenges, and few have done so successfully. Labor prime ministers, it should be said, have had it particularly tough. The first, Chris Watson, had government thrust upon him in 1904 when Australia's second prime minister, Alfred Deakin, resigned on a matter of principle. It was a time when party allegiances were still fluid, and Watson never commanded a parliamentary majority; indeed, some historians do not count his brief administration as a Labor one at all. Deakin resumed the reins but lost the support of Labor in 1908 and Andrew Fisher became Labor's second prime minister.

After being confirmed in the job at the 1910 election, he led an active and progressive government which briefly lost office in 1913, to regain it a year later. But then came the Great War, resulting in the first of Labor's great splits. Billy Hughes, who had forced Fisher to resign in his favour in 1915, tore the party in half over the issue of conscription and Labor faced the first of its long exiles in opposition.

This was broken in 1929 by James Scullin, arguably the unluckiest of all Labor leaders – until now, anyway; the parallels between Scullin and Rudd are striking, if ultimately superficial. Both had big wins in boom conditions against governments that had been in power too long and had introduced draconian industrial-relations measures; in both cases the incumbent prime minister was punished with the loss of his own seat. Both headed enthusiastic but inexperienced ministries in which the desire for long-overdue reform often exceeded political wisdom; and both were hit by an international economic crisis which meant their carefully crafted programs had to be reviewed, modified or postponed. Scullin effectively ceded control of the economy to the ultra-conservative chairman of the Commonwealth Bank, Robert Gibson, and led a one-term government culminating in a second Labor split – in fact a double split, with his treasurer, Joe Lyons, deserting to the Right, and the group led by New South Wales premier Jack Lang heading off to the Left. But the circumstances, as Kevin Rudd would be the first to confirm, were very different. It couldn't happen again.

But as Gough Whitlam might note, it very nearly did. His government, with an even more ambitious reform program, was hit by an oil-price shock which effectively derailed it in its first year of government and set the scene for many of the disasters that followed.

In the meantime Labor had enjoyed its longest period of government to date, although even that had an element of tragedy. John Curtin, the ultimate man of peace who had led the anti-conscription campaign in 1915, became a wartime prime minister, a role he filled heroically until his death just as victory was in sight. His successor, Ben Chifley, presided over the great post-war recovery period, still seen as a Labor golden age, but his defeat in 1949 ushered in the wilderness years and with them the third great split.

Labor saw a patch of light again with Whitlam, but it was a very brief, if spectacular, sunrise; it was left to Bob Hawke, who grabbed the leadership at exactly the right moment, to bring Labor back to a durable form of government. Hawke was the luckiest of all Labor leaders; the times and the Opposition suited him and he suited the electorate. Even the manner of his demise had a touch of good fortune about it; the bad times had begun, but it was his treasurer and successor, Paul Keating, who had to carry the can. Keating restored the Labor tradition of a short government, but a memorable one. Indeed, it was so memorable that it resulted in another eleven years in opposition.

And then – now – there is Rudd. Rudd has made it clear that he is looking forward to a long time in office, but so did both Scullin and Whitlam. And once again it would seem that the world has turned against the new government. Yet Rudd, so far at least, has managed amazingly well. If the polls are to be believed, he is still seen as the best man for the job by an overwhelming majority of Australians. But why? What is it about this repetitive, boring, God-bothering nerd that appeals to the proverbially laid-back, cynical, disengaged public? In any reality-TV contest he would probably be voted The Man Least Likely To Be Prime Minister.

Certainly his popularity has bewildered the political commentariat, who spent much of 2007 insisting that the polling, which consistently showed Rudd coasting towards victory, had to be wrong, that the pollsters and the voters were living in some kind of parallel universe and sooner or later would fall back into the political reality of which they were the custodians. But the voters didn't and they still haven't.

The commentariat, predictably, see this as evidence of Rudd's mastery of spin; since the public consensus remains so far from their own "inside the beltway" views, the public must have been conned. This, of course, contrasts markedly with their verdict during the Howard years: then it was the Left, the so-called elites, who were out of touch with reality. The masses, the majorities who kept re-electing the Coalition, were the ones who had it right. Those who disagreed were stigmatised as "Howard haters."

This now makes the position of the more recalcitrant commentators – Albrechtsen, Piers Akerman, Andrew Bolt, Tom Switzer, for example

– a little difficult: by their own criteria they can be dismissed as mere "Rudd haters."

But the explanation of Rudd's continuing popularity has to be more complicated than successful spin, or that the electorate has somehow just got it right. Rudd's appeal is certainly an unlikely one. He is intelligent and well informed, but no more so than his opponent, Malcolm Turnbull. He has confidence and self-belief, as do all prime ministers; but while these qualities are praised as integrity by some, for others they can suggest smugness and even hubris. He is less sports-obsessed than a Hawke or a Howard, but much more comfortable in the area than a Whitlam or a Keating; however, his attempts at the common touch ("Fair shake of the sauce bottle") do not always come off. His studied use of the internet and of television and radio talk shows has on the whole been successful, but his Christianity is a little too upfront for many Australians.

In public, at least, he is generally softly spoken if somewhat garrulous; he comes across as calm and reasonable, but his attempts at oratory all too frequently descend into management jargon and polly waffle. Overall his persona is more chartered accountant than great war leader. Yet this latter is the role in which he has been cast, and in which a decisive majority of Australians have, so far at least, embraced him. Does this mean that we, as a people, have changed, that we have abandoned our old expectations and ideals in favour of a less exciting, but possibly more reliable model of leadership? Or is it that Kevin Rudd embodies more of the Australian tradition than the commentators are prepared to acknowledge?

It is worth taking a closer look not only at how our present prime minister fits into the proud history of his Labor predecessors, but at how he relates to the range of forces, influences and myths that have formed the Australian ethos. But first, let's look at the situation in which he and we unexpectedly find ourselves. Just where are we and how did we get here?

Back in 2007 it was easy for Kevin Rudd to claim to be an economic conservative, because in the new century there was no credible alternative. With the collapse of the Soviet Union and its satellites and the conversion of China and Vietnam to a kind of market communism, opponents of capitalism had nowhere to go. Socialism was no longer intellectually respectable.

The hardliners could, and did, insist that true economic socialism had never really been tried; that the totalitarian Stalinist and Maoist experiments were little more than perversions of the doctrines of Marx and Lenin. But the hard fact remained that there was not a single successful socialist economy anywhere in the world, and if any further evidence was needed to discredit the ideology, all the triumphant free marketeers had to do was point to the basket cases of Cuba and North Korea.

The historian Francis Fukuyama was so certain of the complete victory of capitalism that he was able to call his paean to it *The End of History* – nothing now could ever challenge the supremacy of Western democratic free enterprise. Echoing him in Australia, Tony Abbott declared that capitalism was simply another word for democracy. On 11 September 2001, militant Islamists made it clear that they did not accept the Fukuyama verdict and were determined to carry history forward in their own way, and Fukuyama was forced to admit that perhaps there was a chapter or two still to be written.

But while the political debate might have a few ideological legs, the economic battle of ideas was over. The market ruled: no serious politician could mount an argument for state control. Socialism was dead and buried. Its death notice had implications far beyond the merely economic. The concept of centralised control of the economy – the public ownership of the means of production, distribution and exchange – was the philosophical underpinning of the entire political Left.

Idealists could still advocate causes such as equality of opportunity and the redistribution of wealth, but they could no longer claim to have a recipe for implementing them. They might look on in horror as governments which claimed to be social-democratic got on with the sale of public assets and the privatisation of resources, but they could offer no coherent program that involved their retention and if they tried, it was dismissed as antediluvian self-interest. Numbers of the former Left deserted Labor altogether and took refuge in the green movement, where economic consistency was not a prerequisite. Those who remained were generally content to rail against what they saw as the excesses of capitalism while being unable to suggest a replacement.

Rudd was firmly ensconced in this camp, at least during the 2007 election campaign. There were occasional hints, especially in his two early essays for the *Monthly*, that he had a vision of a wider, more meaningful commonwealth, but he never spelled it out. He talked of a fork in the road and a bridge too far, and he derided what he called John Howard's Brutopia, but all he really promised was that he would get rid of the hated WorkChoices regime. Obviously there would be changes of emphasis, particularly in the areas of education and climate change, and there would be the long-overdue symbolism of an apology to the stolen generations. But apart from that it would be pretty much business as usual. After all, he was not a revolutionary but an economic conservative.

At least he was until the wheels fell off the free market as decisively as they had fallen off socialism. Deep down, everyone had known that boom times could not last forever; that sooner or later the golden age of economic growth Australians had enjoyed since the recovery from the early 1990s recession would come to an end. But no one had expected the end to be as sudden or as apocalyptic as it threatened to be at the end of 2008. Certainly, in the dying days of the Howard government, the treasurer, Peter Costello, had warned of the risk of an economic tsunami, but he referred to the possibility of the Chinese launching a float of their currency. This would indeed have caused a major upheaval in the international economy, but it would have been temporary and ultimately beneficial as the great trade imbalance between China and the United States levelled out and the prospects for a worthwhile international free-trade agreement markedly improved. Indeed, if the Chinese float had occurred, the effects of the crash that actually came might have been far less devastating.

Instead, some mortgage loans from some American banks went bad and threatened to bring the whole system down with them. The mortgages were euphemistically described as "sub-prime," in much the same way as economists insist on calling a contraction "negative growth." In fact they were basically worthless. And when other bad decisions were factored in, it turned out that the banks were carrying a shitload of what was termed "toxic debt" – in other words, money that was never likely to be repaid. It was the old story, best summed up by Keynes: "If I owe you a pound, I have a problem; but if I owe you a million, the problem is yours."

And the trouble spreads very quickly. The bank has no money to lend for good debts and, in any case, people get scared to borrow; there is a massive collapse in confidence, no one invests, no one spends, and you are in that other splendid euphemism, a recession.

This, of course, is where comparisons with the 1930s and the Great Depression come in, but they should not be taken too far. The present meltdown may be neither as stubbornly enduring nor involve as much human misery as the Great Depression, but it is, as Kevin Rudd among others has realised, far more fundamental.

The Depression was triggered by the Wall Street crash of 1929, when the wave of insatiable greed that had sustained the American stock exchange through the post-war boom collapsed in a panic. As the fore-most chronicler of the times, J.K. Galbraith, points out, this need not have been fatal had the American economy been fundamentally sound. But it wasn't. Galbraith identifies five basic weaknesses: the bad distribution of income, the bad corporate structure, the bad banking structure, the dubious state of the nation's balance of trade and the poor state of economic intelligence.

These failings meant that when the crash in stock values deprived the economy of a major source of spending and investment, it simply couldn't cope; there was no plan B. But this is precisely the point: the weaknesses were, in hindsight, obvious, and could be repaired. A one-off event such as the end of a boom is certainly upsetting, but the system should be able to deal with it. It should not be seen as the end of capitalism as we know it; and of course it wasn't.

The old team of Greed and Fear resumed their merry dance and economic cycles returned to what passed for normal. Sure, there were hiccups, sometimes amounting to major recessions, but nothing that could be called life-threatening. The general belief was that the basic defects that had made the Depression inevitable had been attended to.

The stock exchange was now much better regulated and run as a business. Tax and welfare reform had combined to provide a safety net in the case of economic downturn. The major corporations were now on a much firmer basis: they were backed by real assets instead of being mere bubbles waiting to burst. The banks, too, were more solid and reliable structures: the fly-by-nighters had been eliminated by the very crash they had helped cause. There were, of course, still rogues in the system; it would hardly have been capitalism without them. But they tended to be criminal individuals rather than members of a network of conspirators, and they could be picked off one by one. With the economic rise of China in the 1990s, the balance of payments became a problem, particularly for America, but in general the system of world trade was both freer and better governed than in the past. And, of course, economic intelligence was now an industry in itself: the market had a whole new bureaucracy dedicated to shielding it from shock and surprise. Obviously it couldn't happen again.

But Galbraith, the man who had analysed the problems, believed that it could. Returning to the scene of the crime in 1961, he wrote:

> Even in such a time of madness as the late twenties, a great many
> men in Wall Street remained quite sane. But they also remained

very quiet. The sense of responsibility in the financial community for the community as a whole is not small. It is nearly nil. Perhaps this is inherent. In a community where the primary concern is making money, one of the necessary rules is live and let live. To speak out against madness may be to ruin those who have succumbed to it. So the wise in Wall Street are nearly always silent. The foolish thus have the field to themselves. None rebukes them. There is always the fear, moreover, that even needful self-criticism may be an excuse for government intervention. That is the ultimate horror.

Galbraith saw that the fundamental flaw – a total lack of concern for the consequences of untrammelled greed – had not been rectified. And all the restructuring, all the apparent precautions, all the predictive mechanisms would not work unless there was the will among the participants to take responsibility for their actions. And there wasn't.

During the "Greed Is Good" years, which reached their peak under the benign stewardship of Ronald Reagan in America and Margaret Thatcher in England, the very notion of the market as a human invention designed to serve the needs of the society which designed it was reversed. The market became the reality and society a mere consequence of its operation. (If, that is, the existence of society was acknowledged at all; on one memorable occasion Thatcher declared that there was no such thing.) The market made its own rules and was subject neither to the normal laws of civilised behaviour nor those of economics.

In particular, the ideas of debt and credit lost their original meanings and became almost synonymous terms for the unlimited availability of money. Debts could be consolidated, repackaged and onsold; credit lines could be refinanced, renegotiated and extended indefinitely. Simultaneously the concept of security disappeared altogether: a security was simply a piece of paper (or sometimes not even that) which could be bought and sold. In the real world it might have no value at all, and frequently didn't. But then, the market wanted nothing to do with the real world.

And when the real world finally intruded, the market had absolutely nothing to offer it. Instead, it was forced to embrace Galbraith's ultimate horror: government intervention.

This unprecedented gesture of surrender alone should have made it clear that we were looking at something more than just another episode in the boom and bust cycle. A great many politicians, economists, pundits and astrologers took a long time to wake up to the terrible reality; even as the mighty American automotive industry was giving a new meaning to the slogan "What's good for General Motors is good for the USA" by queuing up in Washington for a taxpayer bailout, there were those who insisted that the doctrine of the laissez-faire free market remained, fundamentally, sound. To his credit, Kevin Rudd was not among them. He saw that the world had changed and was prepared to say so. In the Monthly's first issue of 2009, he stated bluntly: "The great neo-liberal experiment of the past thirty years has failed." Moreover, "Neo-liberalism and the free-market fundamentalism it has produced has been revealed as little more than personal greed dressed up as economic philosophy."

Rudd made it clear that he was not announcing the end of capitalism; quite the contrary. "Not for the first time in history, the international challenge for social democrats is to save capitalism from itself; to recognise the great strengths of open, competitive markets while rejecting the extreme capitalism and unrestrained greed that have perverted so much of the global financial system in recent times."

Needless to say, the extreme capitalists didn't see it that way. Sounding rather like the hardened socialists of twenty years earlier, they insisted that a truly free market had never been tried: no one had been game to give the theories of Friedrich Hayek and Milton Friedman a real go. The problem was not a lack of regulation, but too much of it.

In particular, neo-liberals pointed at the 1977 Community Reinvestment Act of President Jimmy Carter, which mandated banks to look at the financial needs of lower-income neighbourhoods. It did not, of course, compel the banks to issue mortgages to individuals clearly incapable of repaying them, but a lot of banks went into a competitive frenzy and did so anyway, and then repackaged the loans and sold them on to mortgage-holding institutions such as Freddie Mac and Fannie Mae. A bad play, certainly; but according to that socialist rag the *Wall Street Journal*, it accounted in total for just 2 per cent of the accumulating bad debt.

Meanwhile, the masters of the universe on Wall Street continued to invent ever riskier and more incomprehensible tools for gambling on what they appeared to believe would be an ever-expanding jackpot. In 1995 this practice led to the collapse of Britain's oldest trading bank, Barings, when it was discovered that one of its Hong Kong employees had lost zillions in a form of derivative trading called arbitraging, which no one else could even spell. This should have sent some sort of signal, but the only one received by the neo-liberals was that if Barings had lost zillions on derivative trading, then someone else must have made zillions, so let's get into it.

Such an orgy of greed required huge amounts of money and any remaining restraints about borrowing were tossed aside. Credit, the very lifeblood of the market, was irrevocably poisoned. This was the real toxic debt that turned a fall in the market in sub-prime mortgages into a worldwide economic landslide. The collapse of Lehman Brothers, one of the world's biggest merchant banks, in September 2008 was followed by the near-bankrupting of the American motor industry and the entire British economy going into meltdown. Most of the European countries followed, and even Japan, the miracle economy of the last century, the great survivor of the oil-price shocks of the 1970s, suffered a near-catastrophic decline in GDP.

But as late as May 2009, Janet Albrechtsen in the *Australian* was still admiringly quoting a Chilean anglophile and former La Trobe professor named Claudio Veliz, who says it was all due to the *Community Reinvestment Act*, that minor piece of affirmative action from thirty-two years ago. This, presumably, is the state known to the faithful as Invincible Ignorance.

Fortunately, Rudd saw that the problem was a little more basic: just as socialism had failed as a working model, so now what had once been sold in Australia as "economic rationalism" proved not to be rational after all. The war between the competing ideologies was over, but there was no winner: both were injured beyond hope of recovery. But being able to face the awful reality did not mean that Rudd knew what to do about it. Like everyone else he was flying blind; while analogies with the Great Depression worked up to a point, what he had to deal with was both more fundamental and more complex. Nonetheless, some kind of decisive action was imperative. So the Australian government took the orthodox Keynesian approach to economic downturn and, at the end of 2008, hit the economy with what it hoped would be a hefty stimulus to demand: a cash handout to the consumers.

It was undoubtedly better than doing nothing and the consensus of economists around the world was that it was probably a correct first step; but inevitably it didn't work out quite as planned. Over the Howard years the populace had been encouraged to invest, which in practical terms meant to borrow money and use it to get into either the property market or the stock market or both. Indeed, after the sale of the first tranche of Telstra at what turned out to be a knock-down price, Howard boasted that he had turned Australia into the greatest share-owning democracy in the world. At the same time, savings went into reverse: in fact, the only savings most households had were the superannuation contributions paid by their employers under Paul Keating's unfinished scheme, and those too were tied up in property and shares. In the wash-up, Treasury revealed that Howard and Costello had actually sent the budget into structural deficit; even the unprecedented, seemingly endless, wealth of the mining boom had been insufficient to sustain the relentless stream of handouts to complaisant voters.

So when, with the advent of the Great Recession, the bottom fell out of the share market and some house prices went backwards for the first time in living memory, Rudd's beloved working families were hit with a double whammy. Many were paying off mortgages on properties which were declining in value; and although interest rates had plummeted, so too had the worth of the superannuation nest eggs on which they had been relying. Moreover the threat of unemployment, or at least the scaling down of working hours for those in part-time and casual jobs, was suddenly very real. Showing a thrift sadly lacking in the previous decade, they used much of Rudd's bonanza to pay down debt or to save.

In the long term, this was good for everyone; after all, it was the indiscriminate use of credit that had caused the mess in the first place. But in the context of a general fall in demand, Rudd didn't get as much bang for his bucks as he might have hoped. So he gave an open-ended guarantee of bank deposits and whacked off a second stimulus package; in response there came an unexpected surge in retail sales and an even more improbable decline in the rate of unemployment. Optimists started echoing America's banking supremo Ben Bernanke and babbling of green shoots and an early end to the crisis. Hardheads noted that even in the 1930s there had been several minor upward twitches before the economy hit rock bottom, and even after it did, the crawl back up was slow and painful. It was going to be a while yet before the fat lady sang. Rudd found it necessary to pen yet another essay, warning that the real pain was yet to come: the recovery was going to be worse than the collapse. Interest rates would rise, prices of food and petrol would increase, unemployment was still rising, and there would be harsh and unpopular budget measures as the government struggled to reduce the deficit.

But Australians remained determinedly cheerful, and they were buoyed by a set of quite astonishing statistics. When Wayne Swan brought down his second budget in May 2009, the forecast was generally gloomy: unemployment rising to 8.5 per cent, massive deficits for the foreseeable future and debt rising to $13.8 billion. But as the year progressed, the figures stubbornly refused to confirm the official pessimism. By the end of the financial year, Swan and Rudd could boast that on the numbers, Australia was ahead of the rest of the industrialised world: it had the lowest unemployment, deficit and debt of any comparable country and was the only one not in a technical recession. It was a claim they were able to repeat with increasing confidence, both at home and abroad as the year progressed. Suddenly Australia, from being the poor white trash of Asia as Singapore's Lee Kuan Yew had described it just a generation earlier, was transformed into the great survivor. This was important, but almost equally so was the apparent stability of the big financial institutions. Australia had had no casualties even approaching the scale of the collapses in America and Europe. In particular, the banks – the four pillars – had remained rock-solid, even increasing their profits. Critics insisted that they were still bastards and that their success was simply because the government had given them a guarantee, but if this was the case Rudd and Swan could point to them as yet further evidence of the rightness of their policies. The stimulus packages might have been expensive, even wasteful; but by golly, they had saved jobs. Unemployment was nearly a full percentage point below the forecasts. And even if the markets had fallen, the banks had kept the bulk of savings intact. Back in the 1950s, students at Sydney University had a song:

> There'll always be a Menzies
> While there's a BHP,
> For they have drawn their dividends
> Since 1863.

> There'll always be a Menzies
> For Menzies never fails,
> As long as nothing happens to
> The Bank of New South Wales.

> If we should lose our Menzies
> Whatever should we do?
> For Menzies means as much to me
> As Menzies means to you.

Well, BHP had merged with Billiton and the Wales was now Westpac, but apart from that you could substitute "Kevin" for "Menzies" and it would work pretty well in 2009. Back in the days when the original version was popular, Donald Horne wrote his seminal work, *The Lucky Country*. The title was meant to be ironic, but a lot of Australians took it seriously. And nearly fifty years on, it seemed that they still did. This was the first of the Great Australian Myths that Rudd was able to tap: a longstanding and defiant assertion that the place, for all its problems and travails, was closer to utopia than anywhere else on earth.

THE DREAM

In many ways Australia was made for utopianism. It was an untouched land: *terra* not only *incognita* but also, as Europeans saw things, *nullius* – even *vacua* – and therefore a fresh canvas on which the pioneers could draw whatever picture they wished. From the start they showed a preference for the young tree green of a new land over the old dead tree of Europe, which was in any case so remote as to be, for all practical purposes, irrelevant. Geoffrey Blainey's "tyranny of distance" was frequently seen not as a curse but as a blessing. Australia was fortuitously and proudly girt by sea.

The most famous of the nineteenth-century utopians, William Lane, born in England and radicalised in Canada, was a journalist who made his name in Queensland. Already seen as a firebrand, he covered the shearers' strike of 1891 more as a participant than as a reporter:

> And Billy Lane was with them, his words were like a flame,
> The flag of blue above them, they spoke Eureka's name ...

as Helen Palmer's "The Ballad of 1891" records in the musical *Reedy River*. When the strike was broken, he also reported the fate of the ringleaders:

> To trial at Rockhampton the fourteen men were brought,
> The judge had got his orders, the squatters owned the court.
> But for every man was sentenced, a thousand won't forget:
> When they jail a man for striking, it's a rich man's country yet.

Actually they were jailed not for striking, but for inciting rebellion against the crown; like Lane, some of the shearers had dreamed of an ideal socialist society. However, the defeat of 1891 convinced him that his new country was already too politically polarised to give birth to it. So, seeking still more virgin ground, he embarked with 220 of his followers for a patch of unsettled territory in Paraguay. The problem was, as he swiftly discovered, that a perfect society requires perfect inhabitants, and

Lane's mob were too individualistic to comply with his stringent ideas. In particular, they were led astray by alcohol and sex. Lane's attempts to purify them came to nothing; the colony split and its members dispersed, with some returning to Australia and the rest going native.

One of the returnees, Mary Cameron, married a grazier and after a celebrated career as a writer became the first Australian to become ennobled as a Dame Commander of the Order of the British Empire. In 1962 Dame Mary Gilmore was accorded a state funeral in Sydney. Lane ended up in New Zealand, where he resumed his career as a crusading journalist – but this time the crusade was on behalf of Tory imperialism. It was a long way from utopia.

Kevin Rudd would perhaps have shared some of Lane's initial idealism and would certainly have applauded his puritanism. But he would have rejected his extremism out of hand. Repudiating oppressive capitalism is one thing. Embracing authoritarian communism is another entirely, or perhaps they are both sides of a dud, double-headed penny. The failure of Lane's experiment was greeted with relief, but not surprise, by most Australians, who were more concerned, then as now, with their own progress.

But in a more mundane way, the quest for a better way continued. Modern-day Australians have never seen the birth of their nation as much of a cause for celebration, but its architects certainly did: the principals – men such as Alfred Deakin, Edmund Barton and Charles Kingston – talked of federation as a sacred cause, a noble endeavour which would carry the Australian people to a higher form of life. If not quite utopians, they were certainly high-minded idealists.

Of course, they were also politicians and, as such, quite as ambitious and scheming as the present lot, if a great deal more hirsute. Thus the standard story of federation revolves more around the wheeling and dealing between centralists and state powerbrokers than around the undoubtedly lofty aims behind the wrangling. This is partly the fault of our constitution, which is surely the most uninspiring of its kind ever promulgated. Other countries have produced birth certificates extolling the rights of man, the shared humanity of the population, the great freedoms all should enjoy. Australians simply noted the fact that the people of the colonies (well, five of them – the Western Australians only agreed to come to the party later) had, humbly relying on the blessing of Almighty God, agreed to unite under the crown of Great Britain and went on to specify how the administration should work and what powers the colonies were reluctantly prepared to cede to the commonwealth.

Admittedly, the document was prepared as an act of the British parliament rather than as a nationalistic call to arms, but it is hard not to feel that they could have done a bit better. More than a century later the gaps remain to be filled, hence the sporadic pressure for a bill of rights, a proposition which appears to have the tepid support of the government and the implacable antagonism of the political Right, especially those who might be described as neo-liberals. It may thus become another front in Kevin Rudd's ongoing war, although in the present climate a bill of rights, like the republic, will remain what he likes to call a "second-order issue."

So for our generation the constitution is hardly a barbecue-stopper; but for the founding fathers its final acceptance by the mandarins of Whitehall in 1900 was a moment of untrammelled joy. Deakin's diary describes the occasion as splendid and elaborates: "When the door closed upon [the Australian delegation] and left them alone, they seized each other's hands and danced hand in hand in a ring around the centre of the room to express their jubilation." It was the first, and perhaps the only, spontaneous expression of delight the constitution has ever elicited.

Deakin and his fellow delegates were the true believers; others, in the Australian tradition, were more phlegmatic. After the constitutional convention of 1898, George Reid, the New South Wales premier, returned to report to his constituents. Jack Lang summed up the speech thus:

> He started off by saying that he proposed to address himself to the problem as if he was a judge summing up for the benefit of a jury.

Then he carefully enunciated the arguments in favour of federation. Then he switched sides and just as carefully set out the case in opposition. In all he spoke for two hours and when he had concluded his audience was completely in the dark as to whether he was for or against the proposition. From then on he was known as Yes–No Reid.

Others were more straightforward. One of the authors of the constitution, Samuel Griffith, confided that an important reason for his support was personal: he did not like being called a colonial.

But for most, while idealism played a part, it was tempered with the desire for more material benefits. Thus a Tasmanian delegate to the convention: "Gentlemen, if you vote for the bill, you will found a great and glorious nation under the bright Southern Cross and meat will be cheaper; and you will live to see the Australian race dominate the southern seas and you will have a market for both potatoes and apples; and your sons shall reap the grand heritage of nationhood ..." This is surely the approach Kevin Rudd must take as he seeks to cement his position as a leader of both integrity and responsibility. The Australian electorate is susceptible to appeals to its better nature, but seldom forgets the hip-pocket nerve entirely. So when Bob Hawke was preparing to go to the people in 1983 with the slogan, "Reconciliation, recovery and reconstruction," the more practical Neville Wran brought him abruptly back to earth. "It's all very well to go on with all that spiritual stuff," he croaked, "but if those greedy bastards out there wanted spiritualism, they'd join the fucking Hare Krishna." Hawke promptly agreed to tax cuts.

Wran was also spot-on when he addressed Hawke's economic summit. "Delegates," he told the assembled movers and shakers, "this summit is about just three things. Jobs, jobs and jobs." And if there is one thread running unbroken through Australian politics, and Australian Labor politics in particular, it is that. Various writers have identified what has become known as the federation settlement. Paul Kelly popularised the idea of its having five pillars, but in the end they are seen to be only branches spreading from the single trunk of employment. It should be remembered that federation took place in the aftermath of the severe depression of the 1890s, an economic disaster which also gave birth to the Australian Labor Party. This grim memory was clearly in the front of the collective mind that forged the historic compact between capital and labour on which the federation settlement was based.

So we had a commitment to the protection of industry. It was good business: in a country which was yet to impose income tax, tariffs, along with land sales, were the principal source of government revenue. Protectionism could also be seen to be high-minded desire to develop Australia as a self-sufficient nation; even now you can hear the plea that a viable manufacturing sector is vital to Australia's defence, and Kevin Rudd says that he would not want to be the prime minister of a country that doesn't make anything. But this is sophistry. The real reason untold amounts of money have been thrown at Australian secondary industry in general, and the motor vehicle industry in particular, has simply been to protect the jobs of Australian workers. The Coalition suggested this year that Rudd's stimulus program had been a bit pricey: on his own figures each job saved had cost around $260,000 (an estimate which was later revised down to $160,000). But the jobs preserved in the Holden, Ford and Toyota plants through bipartisan policy over the years have been subsidised for a great deal more. Jobs, in the Australian compact, remain literally beyond price.

The second great pillar of settlement, the arbitration system, was in a sense a spin-off, a tool to administer the regime of full employment. While the general principle of a fair day's work for a fair day's pay was accepted by both sides, someone had to decide just what was, in fact, fair. The task fell to Henry Higgins, who stated in his historic Harvester judgment of 1907: "The test to be applied in ascertaining what are fair and reasonable conditions of remuneration of labour under the *Excise Tariff 1906* is, in the case of unskilled labourers – what are the normal needs of the average employee regarded as a human being living in a civilised community?" It was, you will note, taken for granted that the civilised community would provide the average bloke with a job. The Harvester judgment was hated by the free marketeers; a century later it was still being excoriated by the neo-liberal members of the H.R. Nicholls society as irrational mollycoddling, economy-destroying crypto-socialism. But until very recently, the concept of a basic living wage has been a keystone in Australia's employment structures.

The third settlement pillar was White Australia, one of whose principal justifications was the safeguarding of Australian jobs against cheap coloured labour, especially the Pacific islanders who had been kidnapped on so-called blackbirding expeditions to work in the Queensland cane fields. Some apologists, notably Keith Windschuttle, have since claimed that this was its only purpose; no racial element was involved. This is nonsense, as the speeches of the time make clear. Alfred Deakin summed it up thus: "Unity of race is an absolute essential to the unity of Australia." The first prime minister, Edmund Barton, was more explicit: "The doctrine of the equality of man was never intended to apply to the equality of the Englishman and the Chinaman." Isaac Isaacs, who became Australia's first native-born governor-general, spelled it out: "I am prepared to do all that is necessary to ensure that Australia shall be free for all time from the contamination and the degrading influence of inferior races." And in case there was any lingering doubt, the Bulletin asserted: "No nigger, no Chinaman, no Lascar, no Kanaka, no purveyor of cheap coloured labour is an Australian." Race was indeed involved. But, as Labor's first prime minister, Chris Watson, noted, there were also industrial concerns.

As there were even in the fourth pillar: the alignment of foreign policy with Great Britain. This was primarily a declaration of loyalty, but the loyalty was expected to flow both ways. Australia would provide the mother country with troops in her hour of need, and with the raw materials her industry required; but in return we expected a commitment to our own defence, and a reliable market for our goods. Without British trade preferences the position of Australian workers, and particularly agricultural workers, would have been much more vulnerable. The agreement held until Britain joined the EEC in what was seen by many Australians, notably the trade minister, Jack McEwen, as an act of betrayal. For once Black Jack, as he was known, was in accord with the unions, whose members immediately felt the effect.

The final pillar of the Australian settlement was also the most misunderstood: the idea of a benevolent role for the state. This meant that the state should provide the services necessary to support a widely dispersed workforce, particularly water, energy, transport and communication. The state was also in de facto charge of services such as health and education, although it should be noted that these, along with most service provision, remained in the province of the former colonies rather than the centralised commonwealth government. The role of the commonwealth was to oversee the economy as a whole, and that meant providing jobs for all. This was its central, indeed virtually its only, domestic role. It could, therefore, make laws regarding corporations which crossed state borders and it could set terms and conditions for workers who came under federal awards. But a benevolent state was never intended to imply a welfare state; that idea came much later. Of course, if the state failed in its primary purpose – the provision of employment – it had a duty to look after the victims. But their plight was always supposed to be temporary and the treatment distasteful and palliative. Even in the mass unemployment of the Great Depression, the plea was not for susso, but for jobs:

> For dole bread is bitter bread,
> Bitter bread and sour.
> There's grief in the taste of it
> And weevils in the flour.

As so often the poets caught the spirit of the people. In America, the hobos had their vision of utopia in the Big Rock Candy Mountain, where:

There's a lake of gin we can both jump in and the handouts grow
on bushes,
In the new-mown hay we can sleep all day and the bars all have
free lunches;
Where the mail train stops and there ain't no cops and the folks
are tender-hearted,
Where you never change your socks and they never throw rocks
and your hair is never parted.
Oh the buzzin' of the bees in the cigarette trees near the soda
water fountain,
At the lemonade springs where the blue bird sings in the big Rock
Candy Mountain.

All play and no work. In Australia there was no direct parallel, but people
remembered "The Shearer's Dream":

Oh I dreamt I shore in a shearing shed and it was a dream of joy,
For every one of the rouseabouts was a girl dressed up as a boy;
Dressed up like a page in a pantomime and the prettiest ever was
seen,
They had flaxen hair, they had coal black hair and every shade in
between …

The shed was cooled by electric fans that was over every shoot,
The pens was of polished mahogany and everything else to suit;
The huts had springs to the mattresses and the tucker was simply
grand,
And every night by the billabong we danced to a German band.

Our pay was the wool on the jumbucks' backs so we shore till all
was blue,
The sheep was washed before they was shore and the rams was
scented too;

> And we all of us cried when the shed cut out in spite of the long
> > hot days,
> For every hour them girls waltzed in with whisky and beer on
> > trays.

Wonderful conditions, but hard work too; paradise was inconceivable without the job to go with it.

In recent years politicians have had to grow used to the idea of a permanent pool of unemployed, although they have tried to define it away: it has been decreed that just one hour's work a week is to be counted as employment. Methods have had to be invented to deal with the phenomenon, the most determined being the concept of mutual obligation: unemployed persons receiving government benefits are held to be in debt to the state, a debt which must be paid off in the performance of whatever service the state can dream up. The blame has been shifted from the state for its failure to provide work to the unemployed for their failure to procure it. And an unemployment rate of around 6 per cent is now seen to be acceptable, even natural. Fewer than forty years ago, when unemployment reached 1.5 per cent it was considered a national disgrace and was an important factor leading to a change of government.

For Kevin Rudd, such a figure is an impossible dream. But at least he has placed himself firmly in the Australian tradition where jobs are the first priority, with daylight second and the rest well back in the field. It is a position he may find hard to maintain as the recovery gets underway and the problems of dealing with debt and deficit become more potent politically. But as a strategy for dealing with the global financial crisis it is unassailable, especially as his political opponents have no real answer to it. The neoliberals, of course, assert – as they have always asserted – that the answer to unemployment is to break down wages and conditions. They might draw the line at outright slavery, but only just. But the Australian tradition has always held that the compact works both ways: a fair day's work for a fair day's pay, the worker is worthy of his hire. Workers, too, have their pride.

As Rudd recognised, part of the failure of neo-liberalism lay in treating labour as merely another commodity, to be bought and sold as cheaply as possible. Given that the vast majority of consumers are also workers, this meant that the more wages were constrained, the lower the purchasing power of the community. The costs of production might have fallen, but so did the demand for what was produced – or at least the capacity to pay for it. As a result, debt ballooned. It is hardly surprising that the structure eventually collapsed.

So now the search for a replacement – and perhaps even a new, fully employed utopia – is back on. But modernisation has made it more difficult. The original settlement has just about collapsed. White Australia is long gone, as is our political identification with Great Britain – although, as we shall see later, many of the symbolic links remain, and are increasingly a problem for politicians from all sides. Protectionism in respect of trade is now a dirty word, despite the last-ditch efforts of the manufacturing unions to reinstate some form of Australian preference as part of the response to the financial crisis. And the old arbitration system has been modified and modernised over the years. Rudd has restored the central role of an umpire, rejected by the neo-liberals, but most of the former structure has been dismantled in favour of workplace flexibility. This would not have entirely displeased the founding fathers, whose preference was always for conciliation over arbitration, as was made clear in the naming of the original commission. But it has undoubtedly introduced more uncertainty into the system, and into the lives of Rudd's working families.

The compensation for this comes in the final pillar of settlement: the benevolent role of the state. Under John Howard, this was interpreted to mean safety nets and widespread benefit payments, anathematised by the neo-liberals as "middle-class welfare." One of their leading lights, Des Moore, director of the Institute for Private Enterprise, complained: "It is absurd to have 2.7 million, or 20 per cent of the working population, receiving income support compared with only 15 per cent at the end of the 1980s and 4 per cent in 1969. Social assistance benefits now contribute 14.3 per cent of gross household disposable income. This compared with just 8 per cent under Whitlam." The comparison with Gough Whitlam, the bogeyman used by the Right to scare naughty politicians from all sides since 1975, was particularly hurtful to Howard.

Rudd has indicated that some of the Howard handouts will be reviewed and at least rationalised, and the austerity he foresees during the recovery period will provide both an opportunity and an excuse to make a fairly drastic switch. As a politician, he understands how hard it is to remove benefits once they are entrenched. However, his writings and speeches have made it clear that he sees the role of the benevolent state as being more in tune with the thrifty intentions of the Victorian federationists than with the profligacy that developed under John Howard and his quest for middle-class votes. The fair-go principle necessarily entails the premise that the government should spend its limited resources on those who need its help, rather than on those whose help (or votes) it needs. It should be the protector of basic rights and standards for all, not some kind of Santa Claus for favoured groups. Thus Rudd's promise to end the so-called blame game between the commonwealth and the states and bring about an increased centralisation of services. The current system is not only wasteful and inefficient, but, more importantly, unjust and inequitable. Depending on their politics, demographics and position in the electoral cycle, the various governments have different priorities. Laws, charges, benefits, services and subsidies change with state boundaries. Rudd is sufficiently steeped in the Labor tradition to find the differences intolerable. By "ending the blame game" he really means imposing minimum performance standards, particularly in the key areas of health and education, across the country. And here Rudd is appealing to another of the great Australian myths: the idea of an egalitarian society.

Egalitarianism is one of those concepts which instinctively appeals to democrats but is very difficult to put into practice. We have already seen how the founding fathers drew the line at equality of race; it was not until the 1960s that White Australia was formally abolished and although racial discrimination was formally declared illegal in 1975, John Howard happily overrode the law when it came to his dealings with Aborigines. Even today, it is not unusual for recent immigrants – particularly Muslims – to be portrayed as somehow less equal than "real" Australians. Egalitarianism, it seems, remains in the eye of the beholder.

At no time in Australia's history has there ever been equality in the distribution of wealth; the abolition of death duties marked the last gasp of any attempt at equality of outcomes. We are now told that was never the real intention anyway; what matters is equality of opportunity. Australian egalitarianism is the egalitarianism of the fair go. Or at least it is supposed to be. In recent times even that has been subject to certain distortions.

When he was prime minister, John Howard suggested that the fair-go philosophy had had its day; what was needed now was the "have a go" approach, and he made heroes out of those he called "the aspirationals." These were not just people who wanted a better life for their children, as everyone does; they were the go-getters, the thrusters who, perhaps unconsciously, subscribed to the Gordon Gekko mantra of "Greed Is Good." Egalitarianism in the old sense was for the do-gooders and bleeding hearts. Those who still argued that policy should be designed to close the gap between rich and poor were accused of "the politics of envy," but in fact the Howard years spawned a completely new phenomenon: downward envy, where the rich resented any privilege or attention given to the poor and insisted that they deserved additional public benefits. In 2004 one of them summed up the case in a terse letter to the *Sydney Morning Herald*: "The reason the rich need more money than the poor is that they have greater expenses."

There was also a spate of correspondence from those on massive salaries and perks insisting that they were not rich – not really; if people understood what prices in the affluent suburbs of Sydney were like, they would be more understanding. If some executives received astronomical rewards, it was not, as the whingers complained, obscene, but merely the result of international competition – good old supply and demand. And perhaps it was true that the complainants were not really, truly rich – well, not like the Sultan of Brunei is rich. But they *were* in the top 10 per cent of Australians, and all things are relative. It was hard for the average punter to feel much sympathy.

Yet Howard obviously appreciated their plight, and the bulk of his tax cuts went to those at the upper end of the income scale. Electoral bribery in the form of middle-class welfare meant that income disparities did not widen as much as many believed, but there were fringe benefits as well: Howard subsidised private education and private health funds, and gave the rich a big leg-up with superannuation. And on the other side of the scale, he introduced both the GST, which made the tax mix more regressive, and WorkChoices, which once again widened the gap between the top and bottom ends of the workforce.

It was this last that gave Rudd his opening. He did not disparage ambition and initiative, but declared that Howard had gone a bridge too far. We had reached a fork in the road and it was time to restore fairness and balance. And after his election, when the global financial crisis struck, Rudd could and did claim vindication: it had been the greed, the neo-liberal extremism, which had led us to this catastrophe, and people like Howard were to blame. In fact, Howard was a pretty wishy-washy sort of neo-liberal, as Des Moore had pointed out. But he had espoused enough of the rhetoric to make the charge plausible, and many voters seemed happy enough to accept him and his party as the villains in the drama Rudd was scripting. Rudd, of course, was cast as hero, the champion who would restore justice and decency to the Australian scene: the fair go was back.

And the public responded, not only by showing their approbation through the opinion polls but in the most practical way possible. As we have seen, in the wake of the financial crisis unemployment had been expected to accelerate towards double figures; but in fact it barely crawled upwards, so slowly that the economists revised their forecasts down by a full percentage point. Analysis of the statistics showed why: although full-time employment had fallen considerably, part-time employment had risen by almost as much. What had happened was clear: employers and workers had come to an informal agreement that the available work would be shared. Rather than some full-time workers losing their jobs altogether, a great many would accept fewer hours and lower wages. This, surely, was the essence of mateship; a concept John Howard had embraced and indeed tried to appropriate for himself while rejecting the egalitarian ideal in which it had originated. By stating the obvious – that the two could not be separated – Rudd was able to take the conservative position while depicting Howard as a foaming extremist. Once again, he came through as a stable and reassuring force in an uncertain world.

The quest for stability and reassurance is another of the enduring Australian traditions. There is a paradox here. On the one hand, we like to see ourselves as larrikins and rebels, contemptuous of authority in all its forms, sturdily independent and self-reliant. But our history is that of a people who not only have avoided open revolt, but have willingly acquiesced to authority even when it has been blatantly arbitrary and unjust. There have been periods of dissent and even of violence, but they have been infrequent and short-lived. Australians have generally been content to do as they are told, and Kevin Rudd has shown no hesitation in telling them just what that should be. In doing so, he shows that he is aware of the contradiction. Our claim to rugged independence must not be dismissed, but it should not be taken at face value either. Indeed, it offers the clever politician endless opportunities for exploitation.

BEYOND THE CRINGE

The first record I ever owned was an HMV 78 of Peter Dawson singing "Advance Australia Fair." The fruity baritone, who always wore full evening dress to the recording studio, invoked just the right amount of reverence as he intoned the first verse:

> When gallant Cook from Albion sailed
> To trace wide oceans o'er,
> True British courage bore him on
> Till he landed on our shore.
> Then here he raised old England's flag,
> The standard of the brave;
> With all her faults we love her still
> Britannia rules the wave.
> In joyful strains then let us sing
> Advance Australia Fair.

A later verse refers to Australians coming:

> From English soil and Fatherland
> Scotia and Erin fair

– so at least we were portrayed as British rather than purely English. But it was to Britannia we owed our ultimate loyalty.

It is the third verse, which is actually about Australia, which has been adapted and promoted as the national anthem. The second verse is also occasionally sung, but the verse above, which has now been relegated to third, is seldom heard. In a way this is surprising, because most of Australia's national symbols are still redolent with an underlying Anglophilia.

Our flag, of course, is based on the British blue ensign, with the Union Jack as its dominant feature. Our national day, 26 January, marks the anniversary not of our independence, but of our establishment as a British colony. We celebrate the Queen's birthday (well, the birthday of King

George III, but it's the thought that counts) and the British monarch remains our head of state; while a majority of Australians wish to change to a republic, they cannot agree on what kind and prefer the status quo to any compromise.

Our most sacred day of the year marks the anniversary not of an Australian victory protecting our shores but of a frightful military defeat inflicted during a bungled invasion on the other side of the world at the behest of British imperialism. And even the great nationalist William Charles Wentworth, the self-styled native son, was not immune. When he wrote an epic poem outlining his ideals for his homeland, he called it not "Australia," but "The New Britannia." Our colonial period embodied what became known, for more than 100 years afterwards, as "the colonial cringe."

Much of Australian history involves the attempt to shake it off, but even more is wrapped in the pretence that it did not really exist – this is the myth of rugged independence. John Howard never really came to terms with the paradox: he insisted that we did not need to choose between our history and our geography, but it was clear that if the choice had to be made, he was on the side of history. He was forever harking back to past triumphs; for Howard, Australia's sacred sites were the battlefields of Europe. Rudd was thus able to depict him as stuck in the past, while presenting himself as a man of the future, and he has certainly widened the national outlook: Rudd's Australia is a proudly multicultural nation which embraces migrants from all over the world. Its schools and public buildings are more likely to fly the Aboriginal flag, or even that of the United Nations, than the Union Jack. Our attention is directed first to our own region, and next to the Pacific area; Europe has become a second-order issue except where it impinges on multilateral relationships such as the G20, and the connection with Westminster survives chiefly through Britain's titular leadership of the commonwealth. The British tradition remains part of our history, but in practical terms little more. Even so, Rudd is careful to pay that tradition due respect; it has outlasted better politicians than he.

At the end of the nineteenth century the so-called father of federation, Sir Henry Parkes, was keen to weld the colonies into a nation, but not just any nation. "We seek no separation. We only seek to draw closer the bonds of true loyalty, and to continue to share in the rights and privileges that belong to every British subject. We seek a proud place undoubtedly, but it is the proud place of being equals of the best of the British nation and at the same time preserve our Australian identity." In other words, the core value of Australia was to be always British. Certainly, this was the view as the Great War loomed. In his winning election campaign, Labor's Andrew Fisher promised that "our last man and our last shilling will be offered and supplied to our mother country." As prime minister, he pursued his pledge until retirement, and his successor, Billy Hughes, split the party in an effort to conscript Australians for the trenches of Europe. For the new generation of native-born Australians, England was still home.

Indeed, for many, Australian interests were always to be subservient to British interests. In 1931, in the depths of the Great Depression, a young Robert Menzies insisted that Australia's first duty was not to care for its own citizens but to continue to pay dividends to British bondholders: "If Australia was to surmount her troubles only by abandonment of traditional British standards of honesty, justice, fair play and honest endeavour, it would be better for Australia that every citizen within her boundaries should die of starvation during the next six months." Such a stance would now be unthinkable: imagine if Kevin Rudd announced that our first duty during the global financial crisis was to bail out the foreign shareholders of multinational companies that had invested in Australia, and that if we all starved in the gutter as a consequence, well, so be it. If he escaped lynching, he would be placed in a home for the bewildered. So some things have changed; but the idea that Australia should at times be prepared to sacrifice its own interests for those of a powerful patron has not.

Menzies went on to become prime minister and to take his country to war, primarily on behalf of Britain: "It is my melancholy duty to inform you officially that in consequence of a persistence by Germany in her invasion of Poland, Great Britain has declared war on her and that, as a result, Australia is also at war." He later proclaimed himself "British to the bootstraps," and retired, loaded with imperial decorations, his final regret being that he had failed to persuade his colleagues to name Australia's decimal currency unit "the Royal."

Many Australians believe that 1942 marked the end of this post-colonial cringe. Singapore fell and Prime Minister John Curtin stated bluntly: "Without any inhibitions of any kind, I make it clear that Australia looks to America, free of any pangs as to our traditional links or kinship with the United Kingdom."

In the years that followed, the American alliance became paramount and a resurgent Menzies followed the United States into Vietnam, albeit this time claiming that Australia's own national interest was involved. And it was, but not because Vietnam represented any direct threat. Privately, Menzies's deputy, the Country Party leader Jack McEwen, was happy to admit that it was all about keeping America onside, not only as a defence partner but as a trading partner. Menzies's successor, Harold Holt, confirmed the subservient nature of the relationship by adopting the election slogan of President Lyndon Johnson: Australia, he enthused, was "all the way with LBJ." His successor, John Gorton, at least used an Australian reference: "Mr President, we'll go a-waltzing Matilda with you."

The Vietnam adventure ended in tears, but every time Washington needed an ally for an unpopular military invasion, Australia was there. President George W. Bush described Prime Minister John Howard as a man of steel and conferred on him the title of Deputy Sheriff. It didn't have quite the panache of Menzies's ennoblement as Knight of the Thistle and Lord Warden of the Cinque Ports, but the implication was the same: Australia was very comfortable to sit on. The idea of an alliance made sense; during the Cold War and its aftermath Australia had little choice but to seek the protection of a superpower and such protection was bound to come at a price. The question was just how high the price should be. Most Australians accepted the ANZUS treaty as sound policy, but many were unwilling to believe that it meant we had to follow Washington into Vietnam or, worse still, Iraq; such adventures had no more to do with the defence of Australia than had Gallipoli.

Yet the switch from Mother England to Uncle Sam was never a total one. The ongoing popularity of groups such as Australians for Constitutional Monarchy demonstrates a reluctance, particularly among older Australians, to sever their ties completely, and the monarchy itself is still treated with a certain awe. Even during Labor administrations, royal visits have been a pretty big deal, with ardent left-wingers elbowing each other aside in an effort to touch the Queen's glove (size 61/2, incidentally). But by the 1970s such devotees more resembled groupies chasing a celebrity than loyal subjects paying tribute to the crown. And not all showed the same respect: during one such visit in the Whitlam years, an angry delegation of Aboriginal elders arrived at Parliament House demanding to see their prime minister with a demand for land rights. They were met by the president of the Senate, Sir Magnus Cormack, who informed them that they would have to wait; Mr Whitlam was in a meeting with Her Majesty, the Queen. "Well, fuck the Queen," the protesters replied. Sir Magnus, a royalist of the Menzies school, reeled back in horror. It was left to Whitlam to explain later to the delegation that their suggested course of action would have involved a severe breach of protocol. And twenty years later, even that most ardent of republicans, Paul Keating, contented himself with a tactful hand on the royal back.

From the above, it might be concluded that Australia, and particularly its leaders, have an unbroken record of insecurity that can only be assuaged by seeking an omnipotent parental figure in whom to take refuge. Certainly, this is the way a number of other former colonies see us: in particular Indians, who coincidentally also celebrate their national day on 26 January, find it incomprehensible that as late as 1999 we should have voted to retain the British monarchy rather than becoming a republic, as India did in 1947. Clearly we are still political adolescents at best and any pretensions we have to being a truly independent nation might be indulged, but should not be taken seriously. Australia, for all its bluster and bravado, remains an international lackey.

This is a characterisation which would, of course, be indignantly rejected by most Australians, and what's more, they could and would roll out innumerable examples to disprove it. Virtually from the moment they were disembarked from the convict hulks, Irish political prisoners were planning not merely escape, but rebellion against their hated British captors. In 1804, just sixteen years after the inauguration of the prison colony, rebels fought a pitched battle with troopers at Vinegar Hill outside Sydney under the slogan "Liberty or Death." Of course they lost, but the mere fact of the uprising suggests that from the very beginning at least one group of Australians harboured a healthy contempt for authority. Some historians maintain that Vinegar Hill was the real beginning of the Australian republican movement, still active after more than 200 years of false starts.

Just four years later the troopers themselves arrested and imprisoned Governor William Bligh, in what is euphemistically known as the Rum Rebellion but was in fact an act of high treason, a military *coup d'état*. Governor Lachlan Macquarie restored something approaching civic calm, but not much later the dissidents came out in force behind a scurrilous press campaign led by William Charles Wentworth and Robert Wardell urging the recall of Governor James Darling. At least they stopped short of a second coup.

By the 1840s the republicans had been given a new boost by the firebrand Presbyterian John Dunmore Lang, who suggested that the colonists should appeal to the French or the Americans for help to throw off the British yoke. Then came Eureka, at which the rebellious miners unfurled a new national flag, destined, they vowed, to replace the union jack. Once again what started as a protest against a local grievance was transformed into a revolutionary movement with implications for the whole country.

Certainly the authorities saw it as such: the ringleaders were charged not with tax evasion but with sedition. The same action was taken against the leaders of the shearers' strike of 1891, one of the source events that led to the foundation of the Labor Party. And in the meantime, in 1868, a lone Irishman attempted to assassinate the visiting Duke of Edinburgh in Sydney.

It is fair to say that none of these acts of defiance against the crown received widespread public support; indeed, the would-be royal assassin was pursued by a lynch mob, and the colonial secretary, Henry Parkes, set what was to be a far-reaching precedent by using the terrorist attack as the pretext for pushing through parliament the draconian *Treason Felony Act*. Only the Irish Catholics (at whom the new laws were aimed) dared to oppose it, and then not in public; instead they circulated a prayer for Parkes, which read: "If he is bad today, let him be worse tomorrow; and may he be dead, damned and into Hell rammed and may the headstone of Hell be his eternal pillow and that is my prayer for him this blessed holy day."

It suited Parkes and his fellow Anglicans to pretend that all the subversion in the colony was the work of the Fenians, as Parkes called them, and that if they were eliminated, Australia would become an obedient child of the mother country. But as J.D. Lang had shown, and Wentworth before him, Protestants and even Anglicans were perfectly capable of maverick behaviour of their own. Nonetheless, the sectarian divide was an undoubted fact of Australian life and it lasted well beyond federation.

There was opposition to World War I in general and to conscription in particular, but the real militancy came not from pacifists but from the Irish Catholics, who did not want to fight in England's war. One of its leaders was the Catholic archbishop of Melbourne, Daniel Mannix, who then as in later life frequently appeared more politician than prelate. And after the parliamentary divide rationalised itself into an effective two-party system – the conservative coalition on one side and the Labor Party on the other – it was still seen to mirror the sectarian divide for nearly fifty years. It was only the arrival of the wave of anti-communist European Catholics after World War II and the Labor split of 1955 which finally broke down the stereotype, and even then some embers smouldered. It was not until 1956 that Menzies felt ready to appoint a Roman Catholic, John Cramer, to his ministry. And not many years earlier, as a pupil at an Anglican private school, I had been regularly assailed with taunts along the lines of:

> Catholic, Catholic, brave and bold
> Ought to be, ought to be, dipped in gold.
> Protestant, Protestant, down in the pit
> Ought to be, ought to be, dipped in shit.

As a result, I find Kevin Rudd's conversion from Catholic to Anglican mildly amusing. But like so many of his attributes, it is also a political plus, an ecumenism providing reassuring evidence that sectarianism is now dead. Rudd's Christianity, while perhaps a trifle ostentatious for Australian tastes, is of the inclusive, non-threatening variety, in sharp contrast to the fundamentalist zealots of the New South Wales Liberal Party. And of course there were earlier attempts to bridge the divide. During the Great Depression, Henry Lawson was able to write:

> They tramp in mateship, side by side
> The Protestant and Roman;
> They call no biped lord or sir
> And tip their hat to no man.

This was, of course, the same man who wrote:

> So we must fly the rebel flag
> As others did before us
> And we must sing a rebel song
> And join in the rebel chorus.
>
> We'll make the tyrants feel the sting
> Of those that they would throttle.

They need not say the fault is ours
If blood should stain the wattle.

Lawson yearned for the day when the working class would put aside its differences and rise in righteous wrath. And he was no Fenian, but a Protestant immigrant from Norway. In any discussion of the *Bulletin* magazine's two great balladeers, Lawson is seen as the radical and Andrew Barton "Banjo" Paterson as the impeccable representative of the establishment. Yet Paterson too had a streak of nationalism, as can be seen in "Our Own Flag," written shortly after the Great War:

They mustered us up with a royal din
In wearisome weeks of drought
Ere ever the half of the crops were in
Or half of the sheds cut out.

'Twas down with saddle and spurs and whip;
The swagman dropped his swag.
And they hurried us off to an outbound ship
To fight for the English flag.

The English flag — it is ours in sooth
We stand by it wrong or right
But deep in our hearts is the honest truth:
We fought for the sake of the fight.

And the English flag may flutter and wave
Where the world-wide oceans toss.
But the flag the Australian dies to save
Is the flag of the Southern Cross.

If ever they want us to stand the brunt
Of a hard-fought, grim campaign

We will carry our own flag up to the front
When we go to the wars again.

The years between the wars saw the odd outbreak of radicalism and rebellion, but the Great Depression did not produce the mass uprising for which the Marxists had hoped; in spite of Jack Lang and his brother-in-law, Lawson, the workers, on the whole, remained obstinately law-abiding. There were pockets of republicanism and even anarchism, but very little serious antipathy towards Mother England. In fact, the only serious outbreak of anti-British feeling came from the die-hard Tories. When the Australian wicketkeeper Bert Oldfield was felled by Harold Larwood during the 1930 "Bodyline" test series, my grandfather, titular head of the seriously establishment Wentworth clan, stood in his place in the members' stand at the SCG and thundered: "If England were to go to war tomorrow, not a single Australian would fight by her side." And the real revolutionaries came from the political Right: the New Guard, based in New South Wales, was a quasi-fascist organisation which at one stage planned to kidnap Premier Lang and take over the government of the state. In the end the nearest it got to power was when Captain Francis de Groot pre-empted Lang by cutting the ribbon to open the Sydney Harbour Bridge in 1932, but it was a useful reminder that all the subversion did not come from the Left.

It was also a reminder that the authorities consistently failed to heed for the next forty years, during which the Red Menace replaced the Fenian Threat as the preferred enemy within. Had the population been as complaisant and malleable as the earlier version of their history might suggest, they would have fallen easily into line when Robert Menzies held his 1951 referendum to ban the Communist Party. Instead, the proposal was rejected by a narrow margin and the communists continued in their role as a legal and largely ineffective party.

But increasingly, dissent moved away from the organisations and into the universities, workplaces and streets. The communists, while politically impotent in electoral terms, retained a firm base in some of the key trade unions, and in the 1960s the Vietnam War and the re-introduction of conscription radicalised students in an unprecedented manner; it was no longer a matter of a few idealists chanting "Ban the Bomb," but of whole campuses on the march. At the same time the rise of the women's and gay liberation movements provided a new source of direct action.

The brief flowering of the Whitlam government gave hope that real change might be possible through the parliamentary system, but its dismissal seemed the final proof that the establishment would never surrender real power. Far from maintaining the rage, most of the Left lapsed into a period of disillusionment and disengagement, with only the most committed radicals continuing to press the barriers; others found a haven in the green movement. It took the smug oppressiveness of the Howard years to revive any serious resistance, the most obvious and effective examples being the long campaigns against the brutal imprisonment of asylum seekers, children included, and for the release of David Hicks, abandoned by his own government to abuse in a foreign prison.

John Howard felt able to ignore these rumblings because he had recognised something about dissent in Australia: most of it was not really driven by a desire for a better world, or for a more democratic society, or even for a more independent Australia. In almost every instance, under the idealistic veneer ran a strong thread of self-interest. In the case of the convicts at Vinegar Hill, it was obvious enough: end the brutality and the floggings. The troopers who deposed Bligh did so not in the name of freedom for the colony, but simply so they and their patrons could take it over. Wentworth and Wardell had something similar in mind; indeed, Wentworth, the one-time radical, died a hardened Tory. John Dunmore Lang had both personal vendettas and commercial interests at stake when he agitated for independence. The miners of Eureka may have been genuine reformers in the end, but were originally motivated by sheer economics, and the same applies to the shearers of 1891. And most of those opposing conscription have always been those who were themselves at risk, or had relatives or friends who were.

More recently, the self-interest involved in the various liberation movements, in Australia as elsewhere, is obvious, and indeed some advocates, their immediate aims achieved, have lapsed into the same exclusionary behaviour they condemned in others. Even the Free Hicks campaign appeared at times to have more to do with inflicting damage on Howard than with securing justice for Hicks.

And there is another aspect to Australians that most would be reluctant to admit, but which the historian John Hirst regards as perhaps the most firmly engrained of all: the habit of obedience. Australians are used to doing what they are told. This appears to be a legacy not of our convict past, nor of some inbuilt regard for authority, but of a more cynical realism: you can't fight city hall. In the end, the bastards are always going to win, so you might as well cop it sweet. As a result, Australia probably has more nanny-state regulations than any other genuine democracy on earth.

Hirst mentions the traffic-safety rules: seatbelts for drivers and passengers in cars, and crash helmets for riders of both motorbikes and pushbikes. Then there is compulsory breath-testing. He could have added the new, stringent tests for obtaining a driver's licence. And he also highlights our anti-smoking legislation: in most countries the prohibitions on smoking in public venues are simply ignored, but in Melbourne the fans will leave the MCG even on grand final day before lighting up. More seriously, Australians scarcely blinked when Howard effectively handed over control of their national parliament to foreign security services while it was harangued by George W. Bush and Hu Jintao. Some zealots would add our acceptance of compulsory voting as further evidence of subservience to faceless authority. However, our respect for authority breaks down when we can put a name or a face to its agents. Motorists who obediently put their coins in the meter will burst into a torrent of abuse as soon as a parking cop comes into view.

So there is a constant dichotomy: the dutiful citizen, willing to obey and even eager to please on the one hand, and the larrikin outlaw who calls no man his master on the other. Kevin Rudd has obviously identified the bipolar nature of his constituents and is prepared to appeal to both sides. He can be stable and reassuring, a leader willing and able to assume the burdens of his people, but at the same time he can be independent and irreverent. He espouses key institutions, such as the American alliance and the British commonwealth, but he opposed the war in Iraq and is a convinced, if lukewarm, republican. He can be grave and weighty when the occasion demands, but he can also cock a snook, as he himself might put it; he regularly makes cheeky appearances on variety television, talkback radio and the internet. And he has sturdily resisted falling into some easy ideological category. While at different times he has described himself as an economic conservative and a Christian socialist, he remains a bit of an outsider. But not altogether. Rudd is proudly Australian when it matters, and it can matter a lot, because another of the great Australian traditions is a fervent, if understated, nationalism.

Kevin Rudd, former diplomat and Mandarin speaker, is by nature and inclination an internationalist, but he has had no trouble falling into line where Australia's national shibboleths are concerned. Australians are not great flag-wavers and generally find the hand-on-heart style of patriotism exhibited by Americans rather embarrassing. But they have no serious doubt that Australia is the greatest country in the world, nor that Australians are best in the world at everything. Asked to prove this unlikely proposition, some will recall that Australia pioneered votes for women and indeed the universal franchise. An Australian was the third president of the United Nations and the country has produced a disproportionate number of Nobel Prize winners, although few could name more than a couple of them. Others will note that Australians made the first full-length feature film and gave the world the stump-jump plough, the rotary clothes hoist, the motor mower, the wine cask and Vegemite. But almost all will point to the country's pre-eminence in the two fields that really matter: war and sport. These are where Australians really are the tops – or at least they would be if the rest of the world didn't have unfair advantages and often blatantly cheat as well. After all, the bloody Yanks killed Les Darcy and Phar Lap, didn't they? And the Anzacs would have won at Gallipoli except that the bastard British landed them at the wrong place.

The legends of the Anzacs and Les Darcy are powerful ones, and Rudd is right to pay them due homage. Australians like their ceremonies, and while attendance at church is still considered voluntary, no aspiring leader would ever dream of missing an Anzac Day service or a Boxing Day Ashes test. As leader of the Opposition, Rudd often seemed to be shadowing John Howard, both at military ceremonies and sporting events, and his attendance has become even more regular since he moved into the Lodge. Like Howard, he looks an improbable sports fan, but unlike some of his Labor predecessors, he has realised the importance of cultivating the image. Gough Whitlam and Paul Keating both had to be dragged kicking and screaming by their minders to the cricket, the footy and the races; and the New South Wales premier Bob Carr once sat through the first half of a grand final listening to a reading of Marcus Aurelius through a Walkman and then tried to leave at half-time claiming that he thought it was all over.

Bob Hawke, of course, was a natural, and even the august Sir Robert Menzies made a point of timing his frequent trips to England to coincide with the cricketers'. And he expected them to win: no prime minister likes to go down in history as the one who lost the Ashes. Since the days of Bodyline, it has been a given that the only way the Poms can beat us is by cheating, and the same theory has been stretched to include other sports and much more besides. John Howard's petulance when England won the World Cup rugby in 2003 was considered poor sportsmanship by many, but most Australians forgave him; after all, the Wallabies should have won because, as mentioned above, Australians are the best in the world at everything. And as in sport, so in war: look at the Light Horse at Beersheba – indeed, it was General Sir John Monash and his troops who really won the Great War. The diggers saved Tobruk and beat the Japs at Milne Bay, they won every engagement in Vietnam and are the outstanding desert fighters in Afghanistan. Politicians, of course, cannot be quite as crassly jingoistic as this, but they are only too happy to tap into the sentiment. Paul Keating, impervious to sport, kissed the ground at Kokoda and made one of his finest speeches at the tomb of the unknown Australian soldier.

I suspect one of the main reasons Australians revere sport and battle so highly is that both embody the idea of the team: all for one and one for all. And both are great unifiers; they involve all Australians, from the oldest to the newest, on an equal basis. With very rare exceptions, on the battlefields or the sporting fields, race, religion and colour become irrelevant. It is a matter of much self-congratulation within the Australian Rugby League that one of its most respected players is a Lebanese Muslim. In sport and war we find the essence of mateship. And mateship is the highest, the archetypal Australian virtue, worshipped by all politicians in their different, and often self-interested, ways. It is the bond that, throughout our history, has trumped both class loyalty and sectarian difference.

No wonder politicians pay homage to it and seek to appropriate it for their own ends. But it can lead to awkward contradictions: if mateship is supreme, where does that leave the individual? The conservative side of politics has always regarded the interests of the individual as sacrosanct; this is the foundation dogma of the Liberal Party. No one was a more passionate defender of the individual and his right to choice than John Howard; yet, as noted, he also posed as the guardian of mateship and all it stood for. It was a decidedly uncomfortable act of political contortionism.

Rudd, less ideologically constrained, can celebrate mateship without qualification, and does so; his insistence throughout the financial crisis that Australians are all in this together, that we have to be prepared to make sacrifices and help each other, rings far truer than similar exhortations from Howard. Rudd notes the importance of working together in hard times; Australians, after all, are capable of anything and mateship will pull us through now as it has in the past. And he has not forgotten to look back to its origins, and he has found them in the most powerful of Australian myths, that of the bush.

It was in the bush, perceived as alien and hostile by the first settlers, that the need for absolute trust and bonding in a common cause came to be seen not just as a virtue, but a necessity. The bushman, far from the comforts and safeguards afforded by the settlements, had only his mates for company, solace and protection. Mateship was literally the stuff of survival; it was a lesson reinforced when the bushman went to war, and remembered when the digger moved back to the towns.

To many Australians of the present generation, the bush is an old-fashioned, even outdated concept; a hangover from the nineteenth century, irrelevant to those whose Australian roots go back only a generation or two. Nowadays most of us live in cities; two-thirds in the six state capitals and most of the rest in big provincial centres or at least sizeable rural towns. It has become a cliché to note that Australians are among the most urbanised people in the world. But this doesn't mean that we like it. We resist being condemned to high-density living in flats and apartments; if we must live in cities, we at least want a yard of our own. The movement for a sea change or a tree change – an escape to the coast or the countryside – may be a recent development, but the yearning to get away from the rat race is not. Australians may never have been quite sure where to find their utopia, but they know where it isn't. They may not have read William Blake but they share his distaste for dark Satanic mills and that means for city life in general.

The bush, then, is a metaphor for space, freedom and opportunity. Most Australians spend little or no time in it, but they know it is there and that in some not quite defined way it is hugely important that it is. Every town and district has its annual show to celebrate its connections to the bush, and every Easter the bush comes to Sydney for one of the biggest and most popular events of the year. The posher suburbs have pony clubs and hold gymkhanas in imitation of bush entertainment. Townies travel vast distances to attend country race meetings and invest fortunes in vehicles designed to cross the Simpson Desert, even if they never go further than the local pizza take-away. Even our popular culture is not immune: the country-and-western music industry is flourishing and has received a huge boost from Aboriginal performers, and *Crocodile Dundee* and Steve Irwin both achieved cult status.

The very idea of the bush has a powerful hold on the Australian mind, and the bushman was the first, and perhaps the most enduring, of what we would now call our iconic characters. He was not only the explorer, the pioneer who dared to venture into the unknown; he was the settler, the squatter, the tireless patriarch who cleared the stubborn timber and tamed the savage land for himself and his family. But he was also the worker: the station hand, the rouseabout, the drover and perhaps most especially the shearer, of no fixed abode, lumping his swag from shed to shed, unquestionably loyal to his fellows – his mates – but calling no man his master. These two versions of the tradition were, of course, incompatible, and led eventually to the great strike of 1891.

Attempts to reconcile the enemy camps, to combine them into one archetypal bushman, have bewildered historians and legend-makers alike. John Hirst, in his essay "The Pioneer Legend," illustrates the problem. Hirst is an unashamed fan of the early settlers, the rugged individualists (by contrast, another historian, Russel Ward, champions the collectivist view), and uses contemporary poets to back up the view that they were the true heroes. There is no shortage of material: Hirst can even quote the arch-radical Henry Lawson in his cause – his poem "How the Land Was Won" can certainly be interpreted as a paean to the pioneers, although it has more to say about the miseries they endured than about their triumphs. But Hirst regards Lawson's great rival, Banjo Paterson, as his principal witness.

In "Song of the Future," Paterson compares the early explorers with the classical heroes of Greece and Rome; although they were not warriors in the traditional sense – there was, he admits with apparent regret, no hot blood spilt – still,

> nothing in the ages old,
> In song or story written yet
> On Grecian urn or Roman arch,
> Though it should ring with clash of steel,
> Could braver histories unfold
> Than this bush story, yet untold –
> The story of their westward march.

Rudd used such an account of struggle and privation to good effect in his early, Churchillian warnings of the tears and toil that lay ahead when the global financial crisis still seemed to herald Armageddon: our history was one of struggle against apparently insuperable odds, but just as the explorers had fought and conquered the perils of the outback, so too would modern-day resolute Australians triumph over economic adversity. And of course a brighter future lay ahead. For the pioneers it took the form of the idyllic station life, with the squatter kindly and paternalistic, presiding over his fiefdom of permanent and itinerant workers, protecting them – and his own gains – from the rapacity of the city bankers.

It is true, as Hirst notes, that Paterson, in poems such as "On Kiley's Run," has kind words for the squatter. But this was certainly not his final word. In the Saltbush Bill poems, the squatter "Stingy" Smith, owner of Hard Times Hill, becomes a most unappealing villain. The hero here is the raffish, unscrupulous drover:

> The news came down on the Castlereagh and went to the world at
>   large,
> That twenty thousand travelling sheep with Saltbush Bill in
>   charge,
> Were drifting down from a dried-out run to ravage the Castlereagh;
> And the squatters swore when they heard the news and wished
>   they were well away.
> For the name and the fame of Saltbush Bill were over the country-
>   side
> For the wonderful way that he fed his sheep and the dodges and
>   tricks he tried.
> He would lose his way on a Main Stock Route and stray to the
>   squatters' grass;
> He would come to a run with the boss away and swear he had
>   leave to pass;
> And back of all and behind it all, as well the squatters knew,
> If he had to fight, he would fight all day, as long as his sheep got
>   through.

It is tempting to see the Australian political system in terms of the distinction between the squatter – the conservative, protecting his family behind his picket fence, resisting change and enshrining privilege – and the drover – the social democrat always on the move, searching for greener pastures over the next hill. John Howard fits neatly into the squatter tradition, and I suspect Rudd would not mind taking the more adventurous role of the drover. For all his public caution, his espousal of conservatism and his apparent desire to be in control at all times, he shares a measure of Saltbush Bill's single-minded zeal, and he doesn't walk away from a fight. And he certainly doesn't mind breaking down established boundaries if they are hindering his purpose, as the shareholders of Telstra can testify. It has also been revealed that he can swear till the air turns blue, another of the drover's traits. This has never been seen as a challenge to his integrity, any more than was Saltbush Bill's apparent lack of scruple. And the drover doesn't have to be just a brawling rebel – at least not all the time.

So perhaps Rudd has been able to resolve the paradox: he can be the pioneer, breaking new policy ground, beating back the forces of nature and conservative opposition alike; but he can still provide the sense of security and dreams of affluence that were the squatter's reward. Our urbane prime minister's ventures into the bush are infrequent: he makes ritual appearances after disasters such as bushfire and flood and he has dragged his reluctant ministers to regular cabinet meetings in provincial centres as far-flung as Dalby, Walgett and Kyogle. But when he is there, he is a good listener, a trait greatly valued in rural areas, and the fact that he was born in Eumundi, a blink-and-you'll-miss-it Queensland village, is no handicap either.

Without overplaying his bush credentials (which, in fact, are pretty sparse), Rudd has been accepted by his rural constituents as not a bad bloke – even if they're not too keen on his politics. Wisely, he does not try to pretend to be one of them, as Howard sometimes did, going to the extent of wearing an akubra which an unkind cocky claimed made him look like a roofing nail – although even that was considered more suitable garb than the bullet-proof vest he donned to address farmers protesting against his gun laws. Rudd has gone to neither of these extremes, instead assuring bush audiences that, "Rural Australia has been part of my life. I feel at home in rural Australia. I feel welcome there." He has also pursued the idea of Country Labor, a group of rural-based parliamentarians who have tried to portray themselves as Labor's answer to the National Party, a quasi-autonomous branch of the party with a particular concern for those outside the ALP's natural habitat, the cities.

The bush remains special: but in electoral terms it is becoming less crucial. It was ever thus. Lawson saw the end coming with the arrival of the railway:

> The mighty bush, with iron rails,
> Is tethered to the world.

If the decline of rural Australia has been slower and less dramatic than most demographers anticipated, it has been remorseless nevertheless. Over the years the focal point of politics has moved from nostalgia for the outback (the domain of Paterson and Lawson) through acceptance of the outhouse (as portrayed by Ray Lawler and Alan Seymour) to a yearning for the outboard (as ironically celebrated by David Williamson). But the legend lives on, and Rudd is able to use it to engage the cities, with their increasingly green constituency. When calling for action on climate change, Rudd regularly invokes the threat to Australia's natural heritage: the Barrier Reef, the Snowy Mountains, the Murray–Darling basin and our unique flora and fauna are all at risk. Rudd is no noble savage; unlike the Greens leader Bob Brown or his own environment minister, Peter Garrett, he has no desire to spend his spare time in the wilderness. Nonetheless, he is willing to pay due homage to Paterson's Arcadian vision of the drover in his classic "Clancy of the Overflow":

> And the bush has friends to meet him, and their kindly voices
>   greet him
> In the murmur of the breezes and the river on its bars,

And he sees the vision splendid of the sunlit plains extended,
And at night the wondrous glory of the everlasting stars.

Rudd would also acknowledge that there was another side to Clancy
which Paterson does not mention. In spite of the poet's assertion that no
blood was shed in the pioneering days, actually quite a lot was; it's just
that very little of it was white man's blood. For Paterson, Indigenous Australians were barely perceptible; if seen at all, they were lovable clowns,
figures of fun, not part of the real narrative. But, as we now realise, their
story should not be left out. Here is Clancy from the other side:

> He was poisoning the water when he chanced upon a slaughter
> So he joined in patriotically to massacre and rape
> And he sees the vision splendid of the native problem ended
> And a land made safe for cattle from Tasmania to the Cape.
>
> In my genocidal fancy visions come to me of Clancy
> With a gin across his saddle and her children in pursuit;
> As he leaves behind their crying he tots up the dead and dying
> And he calculates his bounty and gets ready for a root.
>
> With commendable persistence Clancy follows the resistance
> And you'll find him in the rearguard with the priests and their Te
>   Deums.
> While the troopers do the shooting Clancy rides behind them,
>   looting;
> There's tjuringas for collectors and some heads for the museums.
>
> And when he meets a Jacky Clancy sometimes offers baccy,
> And many other presents to improve the shining hour.
> When his cobbers call him silly, he just smiles and boils his billy
> For there's measles in the blanket rolls and strychnine in the flour.

And a firm but friendly parson thinks he'll try a little arson
To exorcise the dreaming with his candle, book and bell;
His redeemer loudly praising, he sets all the gunyahs blazing
To civilise the heathen with a touch of Christian hell.

As he contemplates the scene he can remember Truganini
And Pemulwuy and Banelon and others of their kind
And on gentle summer breezes he can sense the new diseases
That will carry their descendants out of sight and out of mind.

And the sturdy stockhorse whinnies as he tramples piccaninnies
And the rider cracks his stockwhip at the ones who run away
And above the odd death rattle he can hear the lowing cattle
As the drover brings them into camp to end a perfect day.

A blemish, John Howard called it. But we should not judge our fore-bears by today's standards. They meant well, they thought they were doing the right thing. And whatever mistakes they made, we – or at least he and his government – had nothing to apologise for. Howard rejected what he called the black armband view of history and claimed a special relationship with the farmers, a "compact," in fact, and happily tore up Australia's *Racial Discrimination Act* to pass legislation guaranteeing their exclusive property rights when the High Court found, in the *Wik* case, that in some cases Aborigines might have retained a form of co-title to the land the pastoralists – the settlers and the squatters – leased. The move was good politics: Howard needed to mend his fences with his rural con-stituents in the wake of the gun-control legislation, and his black con-stituents could be dismissed as collateral damage. Howard cleaved strongly to another perceived foundation of the Australian tradition: there are no votes in Aborigines.

Many of his predecessors have tried to change the perception: history is replete with political gestures designed to gain sympathy and support for those now known as the first Australians. Harold Holt ran the historic referendum of 1967 which removed constitutional discrimination against Aborigines and allowed the commonwealth to legislate on their behalf – or, as Howard proved, to their detriment. Gough Whitlam made land rights a reality when he poured sand though the hands of Gurindji leader Vincent Lingiari. Malcolm Fraser carried land-rights legislation in the Northern Territory through to completion and implemented the *Racial Discrimination Act*. Bob Hawke set up the Aboriginal and Torres Strait Islander Commission as a national Indigenous forum and announced reconciliation as a priority. Paul Keating's Redfern Park speech accepted responsibility for the damage done to Aboriginal living conditions and culture and promised reparation. And Kevin Rudd made the apology to the stolen generations refused for so many years by Howard and restarted the reconciliation process Howard had blocked.

But he also continued, in a slightly watered-down form, Howard's single initiative in Aboriginal affairs: the Northern Territory intervention. This blitzkrieg was launched without warning or advice; the *Racial Discrimination Act* was again suspended to enable what amounted to martial law to be declared over selected settlements in the Northern Territory. The leftist policies of self-determination backed up with generous but often ill-directed welfare were pronounced failures; in their place Howard fell back on the time-honoured practice of paternalism, although in a form which was perilously close to brute force. His immediate *casus belli* was a spate of revelations about child abuse, but the broader motive was to break the cycle of poverty, violence and dependence.

Rudd basically approved of the aim, but, like many Aboriginal leaders, was unhappy about the complete lack of consultation with those affected. He promised more inclusion and the restoration of the *Racial Discrimination Act*; he also set himself a bold timetable in which to achieve his policy of closing the gap between the living standards of black and white Australia. But so far very little has been achieved. It appears that the degradation of Aborigines is to be seen as another continuing thread in the Australian fabric.

It is one that Rudd, like many of his predecessors, would love to remove. Not only is it a terrible blight on Australia's international reputation at a time when Rudd is seeking to reposition the country as a serious player on the world stage, but he genuinely believes that we can and should do better. There are echoes here of Whitlam's great promise of 1972: "We will legislate to give Aborigines land rights, not only because the case for them is beyond argument, but because all of us as Australians are diminished while the Aborigines are denied their rightful place in this nation." Rudd would dearly love to recapture the heady optimism of those days, and one of the ways he is trying to use and modify the Australian tradition is to restore a sense of idealism; to persuade the so-called aspirational voters that there is more to aspire to than just moving up to a bigger McMansion. While not rejecting materialism as such, Rudd believes that the unrestrained pursuit of it was one of the root causes of the financial crisis and is determined to restore a balance. Unlike Howard, he does not see the accumulation of wealth and its trappings as an end in itself but only as a means to a fuller life, as shown by his opposition to the way WorkChoices traded off entitlements such as holidays and long-service leave for increased pay. Rudd may have turned the phrase "working families" into a cliché, but he has always made it clear that there is also a place for leisure. And as we have seen, one of Howard's boasts was that by selling Telstra he turned Australia into a nation of share owners. Rudd, in contrast, is happy to see the value of Telstra shares fall if this achieves a better outcome for national broadband coverage.

And in pursuit of long-term improvements to the system, he is prepared to accept a period, albeit a brief one, in which living standards might actually fall. He has warned that this is likely to be the case during the recovery from the financial crisis, with prices and interest rates rising as the government puts a lid on services and seeks to repay its debts. This, he believes, is a price worth paying for Australia's relatively soft passage through the downturn itself.

The polls attest to the widespread feeling among voters that Rudd has handled the crisis pretty well; like Winston Churchill, he has shown himself to be the wartime leader the occasion demanded. The question now is whether, unlike Churchill, he will be able to manage the difficult transition back to peace and normality. By the second half of 2009, it seemed that surviving the global financial crisis might have been the easy bit – at least in political terms.

A consistent criticism of Rudd, from supporters as well as from opponents, is that he has failed to construct a coherent political narrative for his government. He has done pretty well in dismantling John Howard's version of Australia, but he has not replaced it with one of his own. I think this judgment is a little unfair; Rudd has in fact embraced a great deal of the Australian tradition, in terms of both its myths and its values. But he has done so in a characteristically unobtrusive manner, thus blurring both the difference and the similarities with Howard's own narrative.

Howard emphasised a narrow and selective view of the nation's history. His Australia was an idealised look backwards: a country which was a product of the West, European – in fact British – monarchist, untroubled by cultural differences, a society where the people accepted their assigned roles:

> The rich man in his castle,
> The poor man at his gate,
> God made them, high or lowly,
> And ordered their estate.

as Howard would no doubt have sung in the churches of his youth.

It had a proud military and sporting tradition, and that was enough. The so-called blemishes could be, and were, disregarded. We were happy to trade with the countries around us, but that did not mean making them part of the family; we abided by the proverb that strong fences mean good neighbours. Our real ties were with the white Anglophone nations. This was the way it always had been, and was meant to be.

It was a simple and easily marketable story, and Rudd has been clever enough not to discard it completely. Instead, he has accepted some of the core ideas, but he has built on them, using them as the foundation for a more complex and inclusive structure. Rudd's Australia is still very much a work in progress, but it places the nation as an active and innovative participant in the immediate region, with interests that run much more widely than the merely economic. It is a country which continues to acknowledge and celebrate its Western heritage, particularly regarding democratic politics and the rule of law. But it recognises that immigration has eroded the British connection to the point of irrelevance for many, and that globalisation is likely to complete the process. This it regards not as a threat but an opportunity, and it welcomes the chance for greater involvement and wider horizons. Australia's emergence as a modern multicultural nation with a stable democratic history makes it ideally positioned for an enhanced, even a pivotal role in the changes that will flow from the global financial crisis and Rudd has thrown himself into the vacuum left by the implosion of the neo-liberal ethos. His campaign to secure a seat for Australia on the United Nations Security Council has been dismissed by his critics as hubristic symbolism, but the same cannot be said of his embrace of the G20 group. The meeting in Pittsburgh in September was truly a time of transition, a turning point in history.

The acceptance by all the major players of the role of the G20 as a rule-maker for the conduct of the financial systems of member nations quite literally ushered in a new world economic order. And this was not some kind of Orwellian nightmare in which a conspiracy of plutocrats (or Jews, or Masons, or Martians) use their might to enslave the wretched of the earth, but a genuine democratisation which directly includes two-thirds of the world's population and indirectly gives a voice to the rest.

The London meeting of the G20 in April proved that the new organisation could actually work; that the diverse array of interests could cooperate in reforms to a system in desperate need of them. Now the process has been formalised and we have a long-overdue representative body with both the power and the will to lead the world out of the global economic crisis and towards a better and fairer model of interdependence for the future. Unsurprisingly, the Australian media have made much of the fact that Australia, as an active member of the club, has a seat at the top table, and this is indeed a cause for rejoicing. But far more important is the part Australia played in its construction, which is a matter for genuine and bipartisan pride.

The G20 was born out of the G7, the clique of big, rich nations that emerged as a result of the oil-price shocks of the 1970s. It was centred around the Atlantic: Britain, Germany, France and Italy from Europe, and the USA and Canada from the Americas. Japan was included as the only developed economy successfully to manage the crisis. After the Cold War ended, Russia was added as a reward for converting to capitalism, and that was the G8. It persisted long past its use-by date, although there was some recognition that the world was changing; finance ministers, including Peter Costello in a rare moment of activism, formed the first version of the G20 when it became obvious that the developing economies were becoming too big to ignore. China and India were included as a matter of course, and Indonesia and South Korea joined them to represent the new power base in Asia. Argentina and Chile brought South America into the picture, and South Africa and Saudi Arabia moved the group into new territories. In the name of inclusion, Turkey, Mexico and Australia were given guernseys, and to placate the Europeans (who rather resented the presence of so many parvenus) an extra position was created for the European Union as a whole. Thus the G20.

Its founders from the G8 intended it only as an economic talk shop, not as an implementer of policy and certainly not as a gathering place for heads of government. But the global financial crisis gave it new life. The G20 coordinated stimulus plans worth a staggering US$5 trillion (that's $5,000,000,000,000) and another trillion for emergency aid where it was needed. It didn't avert the crisis, but it certainly made a difference. The London meeting, which was attended by several presidents and prime minsters, including Kevin Rudd, effectively ended the panic and began the movement towards recovery. The comparison with the G8, which did nothing useful at all, could not be overlooked.

And it wasn't; certainly not by Rudd, who recognised the opportunity to consolidate and expand the group's role to make it a permanent economic planner, coordinator and watchdog. He had powerful allies in China and India, who felt the role was theirs by right, and unsurprisingly the other smaller nations were eager to enhance their own positions. But the Europeans resisted. France, in particular, did not want the new group institutionalised, and argued that if the G8 was to be expanded at all, fifteen should be the cut-off point.

By what was probably not a coincidence, this would have excluded Australia: France did not want the Anglosphere to gain another active voice. However, Barack Obama swung his support behind Rudd, and the deal was done. It was a triumph for Rudd, and for effectiveness, good sense and fairness.

It also gave Rudd a platform to spell out, for the first time, the regulations he saw as basic for the reform of capitalism in the wake of the GFC: the licensing of systemically important banks, improved financial adequacy, reward for performance rather than greed, realistic valuation of assets and better prudential analysis. These may or may not be adopted in whole or in part, but at the very least they provide a coherent alternative to neo-liberalism. One suspects Galbraith would have approved.

The consolidation of the G20 is a massive achievement in its own right. And it is a pointer to further international reform. Unlike John Howard, who preferred bilateral meetings, and not too many of those – unless, of course, they were with George W. Bush – Rudd is a strong believer in multinational relationships and organisations, and one of his targets has long been the International Monetary Fund. This dinosaur is precisely the kind of institution loathed by the Left, a neo-liberal throwback under the effective control of the bankers of Washington. Although it has 186 countries as nominal members, only the US has a power of veto; with more than 16 per cent of the voting power, it can stymie the 85 per cent needed for a binding resolution. By contrast, Japan, as economy number two, controls just over 6 per cent, China 3.5 and Australia 1.5.

165 countries – nearly 90 per cent of the membership – have less than 29 per cent between them. Clearly this has to change, and Rudd, from the platform of the G20, is determined to change it.

And after the IMF, the United Nations itself: the Security Council, like the G8, needs to be brought up to date; expanded and made more representative to reflect the modern world. The General Assembly, with 192 members, is obviously hopelessly unwieldy, but at least the bloated bureaucracy that goes with it can be streamlined. These may be ambitious goals for the leader of a small-to-middling country at the arse-end of the world, but a couple of years ago the G20 looked an impossible dream. With determination and the right friends, it has become a brilliant reality. Yes, we can.

In Manning Clark's terms, Rudd is an enlarger where Howard was a straitener. Rudd's Australia is expansive and outgoing, whereas Howard's was always symbolised by the picket fence. But this does not make Rudd a radical; his instincts remain those of an old-fashioned Whig, or even what one American described as "a modern progressive – that's a fella that stumbles forward every time somebody shoves him." The only reason his policies have a whiff of the future about them is that Howard's were so firmly grounded in the past. Howard described himself as a conservative, but in fact he was reactionary; he yearned to take Australia back to a largely imaginary past. When Rudd takes on the conservative label, there is much more reason to believe him.

In spite of his vaulting ambition and his considerable achievements working within the system, he has shown no inclination for revolutionary change even when confronted by problems as far-reaching as the global financial crisis and climate change. Indeed, on the latter he appears to have all but abandoned what he once saw as the great moral, political and economic challenge of our times to the forces of ignorance, denial, self-interest and sheer bloodymindedness. Although he has talked about a different approach, domestically at least he has taken very small steps towards one: the only substantial parts of the Howard legacy he has sought to reverse are WorkChoices and the Pacific Solution, and even there he has retained elements of both in his own policies. Rudd can convincingly maintain that he has done no more than restore the status quo, surely the ultimate conservative position. And he has done so by appealing not to some new order or manifesto for the future but to the enduring myths and values of the past. Here he has the huge advantage of leading a party whose history and traditions run parallel to that of the country itself. Labor's roots were in place well before federation. The conservative forces did not cohere until 1909, and since then have gone through a number of different incarnations including two under the leadership of Labor apostates (and those do not include Brendan Nelson).

The political scientist Tim Soutphommasane, in his recent book *Reclaiming Patriotism*, argues that just as the conservative side of politics took political possession of the idea of competent economic management, so it did with the symbols of national pride. In neither case was the grab justified by the facts; it was the Hawke–Keating years that actually set up the modern Australian economy, and under Howard patriotism often seemed to descend to the level satirised by Barry Humphries, who once defined xenophobia as "love of Australia."

Soutphommasane suggests that just as Labor is regaining confidence in its economic credentials, it is time for progressives to set their own stamp on nationalism; to show that it can be more than the crude stereotype Howard used to dog-whistle his warning about the outside world. Patriotism is, after all, very much a Labor virtue; John Curtin is celebrated as Labor's greatest leader, and also the supreme Australian nationalist. The idea is one that should have a visceral appeal for Rudd, who began his ascent to power by insisting that the Tories had no monopoly on Christianity. And certainly by embracing Australian tradition as he has, he has made a solid start. The narrative is yet to take on a plot line that will pull the public in as eager readers, but the basic structure is well and truly laid down. A hint of where it might go lies in Rudd's August launch of Tom

Keneally's picaresque history of Australia. Rudd praised the first volume of *Australians* for its warts-and-all approach to this well-worn subject; its recording of shame as well as glory, absurdity as well as courage. Rudd's overall verdict, of course, is that we have done good, played well. But it is not an unqualified verdict: the line he is pushing is that we can learn from history and improve on it. We must continue to work towards the vision splendid and he has a blueprint for us to follow.

There are echoes of Gough Whitlam in the methodical way Rudd has gone about this, and indeed in his agenda, education, health, social justice and community issues predominate. Trevor Cook of Sydney University has noted that a majority of the new Labor members who came in with the triumphant election of 2007 share his priorities, at least judging from their maiden speeches. And looking further afield, the electorate might agree: for a generation for whom the Cold War is a fading memory and for the continuing influx of migrants anxious to learn the customs of their new home, the social contract with which Whitlam won office could have considerable appeal and relevance. But in every other way – except, perhaps, his idealism – Rudd has eschewed the example of his legendary predecessor. Whitlam charged into office like a tornado, scattering legislation in all directions. Rudd has spent much of his first term in setting up inquiries, convening meetings and generally preparing the ground for what he obviously intends to be a long time in office. The exception, of course, has been the reaction to the global financial crisis, which was tackled hard and fast, and, it would seem, very effectively. By contrast, the government's caution in other fields has been almost painful.

Rudd has claimed that in spite of the distraction of the financial crisis and its still unwinding consequences, his program is still on track and that his election promises have all been, or will be, fulfilled – at least as far as an increasingly erratic and hostile Senate will allow. But in practice the scorers have not been overworked. WorkChoices is gone, but its replacement is requiring an inordinate amount of fine-tuning. The education revolution is underway, but progress is a lot slower and more sporadic than was promised. The national broadband network is little more than a couple of holes in the ground in Tasmania. The health impasse with the states, the archetypal example of the blame game, seems as deadlocked as ever, with deadlines already missed. And of course the great issue of Aboriginal disadvantage, which Rudd invoked at the very start of his prime minister-ship, remains a reason for national shame. These are the nitty-gritty of government.

It can fairly be argued that in the first couple of years of Rudd's admin-istration they have been overshadowed by the financial crisis and, more recently, by the intransigence of the Opposition over the emissions trad-ing scheme, both unquestionably crucial and urgent issues. And in differ-ent ways both will be dominant in 2010 as well. But Rudd will want more than the sense of ongoing crisis management, however successful, to take to the voters on election day. The way things are looking, there will not be very many projects actually finished and working by that time. So Rudd and his colleagues will have to rely largely on intangibles, and it is here that his ability to compose and articulate a convincing version of the Australian story could be vital.

This view will be dismissed out of hand by much of the media, who generally regard what was once derided as "the vision thing" as little more than elitist wankery. When they talk about a narrative, they mean something that can be expressed in a thirty-second television advertise-ment, or better still in a single memorable phrase: "We will decide who comes to this country and the circumstances in which they come." But I suspect this contempt for Australia's deeper mythology is one reason so many economically oriented commentators have struggled to understand the appeal of Kevin Rudd.

He does not have the aura of Alfred Deakin nor the down-to-earth charisma of Ben Chifley; he is not a war hero nor an Olympic medallist. He bears no resemblance to the shearers of Barcaldine nor the miners of Eureka. Yet there is a sense in which he comes across as the heir and successor to all of them. For all his nerdiness and prolixity, there is something very Australian about him, and the voters recognise it. In a totally unexpected way, Rudd has given them back their Lucky Country – and this time not in a spirit of irony, but one of self-belief. Just as all the economic and ideological certainties were crumbling, he took them back to the bedrock of their legends, their values and their dreams – to a country which has never really existed and probably never will, but which is the Australia to which they want to belong. This is Kevin Michael Rudd's secret. Some see it as integrity, but many more simply feel that they can trust it – Kevin from Queensland really is there to help them. It sounds corny, even kitsch. But by golly, it wins elections.

IS NEO-LIBERALISM FINISHED?

2009 Quarterly Essay Lecture

Robert Manne

On the eve of the 1979 British election, the Labour Party prime minister, James Callaghan, fell into conversation with the head of the Downing Street Policy Unit, Bernard Donoghue. Donoghue thought the opinion polls might be improving for Labour. There was still a chance of victory. "I should not be too sure," Callaghan replied. "You know there are times, perhaps every thirty years, when there is a sea change in politics … I suspect there is now such a sea change – and it is for Mrs Thatcher." Exactly thirty years later, another Labor prime minister had a similar thought, although this time it was inspired not by pessimism but by hope. "From time to time in human history," Kevin Rudd argued in his *Monthly* essay earlier this year, "there occur events of a truly seismic significance, events that mark a turning point between one epoch and the next, when one orthodoxy is overthrown and another takes its place … There is a sense that we are now living through just such a time." Rudd characterised the thirty-year-old orthodoxy that he thought was in the process of being overthrown as "free-market fundamentalism, extreme capitalism, excessive greed." The orthodoxy had been called, in different countries and at different times, "Thatcherism," "Reaganomics," "Rogernomics" and in Australia, "economic rationalism." In his essay, Rudd used its most common name, "neo-liberalism." As will I.

This essay is concerned with three closely related questions. What has been the impact of the neo-liberal idea in the country where its influence has been strongest, the United States? Does the ideology of neo-liberalism, as expressed in recent US economic history, bear responsibility for plunging the world into what is coming to be called the Great Recession, the most serious economic downturn since the Great Depression? If so, is it likely that the era of neo-liberalism is finally drawing to its end?

The historian Eric Hobsbawm has called the thirty-year period that followed World War II capitalism's "Golden Years." This era was marked by very significant economic growth throughout the West; by even more significant levels of international trade; by the virtual elimination of both unemployment and inflation; by the apparent end of capitalism's regular cycles of boom and bust; by the emergence of the so-called mixed economy, where parts of the economy were dominated by private enterprise and other parts, such as energy and transport, by the public sector; where both trade unions and big business were regarded as entirely legitimate economic actors; and where expenditure on the welfare state came to absorb a very considerable and apparently ever-growing part of every Western nation's wealth. The dominant economist of this era was John Maynard Keynes. He taught an entire generation that governments had it within their power, essentially through fiscal policy, to overcome the twin evils that beset the capitalist economy: inflation and unemployment. When economies were "overheating" and inflation therefore threatening, governments could tighten public spending. When the economies were heading towards recession and the problem of unemployment loomed, governments could borrow and increase their public spending. An Australian economist formalised this theory in the so-called "Phillips Curve."

For thirty years Keynesianism appeared to work. Because of the Great Depression, mass unemployment was now regarded as an unmitigated evil. If it should ever return, the political elites feared that domestic communist parties associated with the Soviet Union, the external enemy of the West, would be the beneficiaries. In combination, the memory of the Great Depression and the present fear about the possible attractions of communism for the Western working class provided the intellectual basis for the Keynesian social-democratic consensus which helped civilise and stabilise capitalism.

The most important enemies of Keynes were the economic liberals who, in 1947, had organised themselves into a high-level intellectual association known as the Mont Pelerin Society. Its most important members were Friedrich Hayek and, later, Milton Friedman. The purpose of the Mont Pelerin Society was to keep the liberal idea alive in what was seen as the era of communism on one side of the iron curtain and of Keynesianism on the other. The old-style economic liberals regarded communism and Keynesian social democracy as different versions of a single, wholly negative trend. Sometimes they called this trend socialism; sometimes collectivism. By embracing collectivist policies, such as Keynesian demand management or the creation of substantial welfare states, the economic liberals believed that Western societies had, through intellectual error, set out upon a path that would lead eventually to the nightmare of the totalitarian state. They thought that the social-democratic countries of north-west Europe, such as Sweden or the Netherlands, had already advanced a long way down that road.

The further advance of collectivism was not, however, inevitable. The economic liberals believed in the power of action and ideas. They were inspired by the insights of their enemies. They adopted as their slogan the famous concluding words of Keynes' *General Theory of Employment, Interest and Money* – "Madmen in authority, who hear voices in the air, are distilling their frenzy from some academic scribbler of a few years back ... the power of vested interests is vastly exaggerated compared with the gradual encroachment of ideas." What the British Fabians had once done to spread the idea of socialism, through the permeation of institutions, they would now do to spread the liberal idea. The economic liberals in both Britain and the United States created important think-tanks; in the universities they trained a new generation of academic economists; beyond the academy they converted journalists and politicians to their cause. The process of permeation in Britain has been brilliantly analysed in a book called *Thinking the Unthinkable* by Richard Cockett, a sympathetic historian.

The economic liberals always believed that Keynesian social democracy was doomed. Its fundamental weakness was the debilitating inflation its policies ultimately would not be able to avoid. A German economic liberal, Ropke, explained the link between Keynesianism and inflation in this way: "A policy which ... sees unemployment ... as sufficient reason for increasing 'effective demand' is necessarily tantamount to a policy of constantly inflationary pressure ... The social evil of partial employment will then be [replaced] by the even greater evil of general inflation." In his *Constitution of Liberty*, Hayek explained somewhat differently why the Keynesian experiment would inevitably collapse. Keynes thought that because of the power of trade unions the struggle to reduce wages was too politically painful to be contemplated, even when necessary to maintain full employment. Keynes, therefore, according to Hayek, "concluded that real wages must be lowered by the process of lowering the value of money ... In practice this necessarily means that each separate union ... will never cease to insist on further increases in money wages and that the aggregate effort of the unions will thus bring about progressive inflation." Hayek believed that because of the inflationary threat, the Keynesian social democrats were holding what he called "a tiger by the tail."

In 1974 and in the years thereafter, following almost thirty years of prosperity, all Western economies were quite suddenly afflicted by high levels of both inflation and unemployment, for which a new term, stagflation, had to be invented. The arrival of stagflation was a critical moment in Western post-war history. On the one hand, the Keynesian paradigm, at least as popularly understood, apparently collapsed. Within the para-digm, inflation and unemployment were the alternative illnesses to which a capitalist economy might be prone. Within it, the idea of stagflation was as conceptually confusing as the idea of freezing fire or burning ice. On the other hand, the arrival of stagflation gave the economic liberals their chance.

Ever since the Keynesian social-democratic consensus had crystallised in the early post-war years, the economic liberals had been waiting for this inflationary crisis to arrive. They were the party-in-waiting. As Milton Friedman made clear in his Nobel Prize acceptance address, the economic liberals did not now succeed purely or even mainly through the power of their ideas. They succeeded because, after the arrival of stagflation, brute facts about the ills now afflicting all the capitalist economies of the West seemed to vindicate what they had long claimed. The awarding of the Nobel Prize for Economics not only to Friedman but also to Hayek in the mid-to-late 1970s was one sign of change. Another was the election of the Thatcher government in Britain in 1979 and the Reagan administration in the United States in 1980. In Britain and the United States, the struggle against inflation and the power of trade unions now began in earnest. Just as history sees in the October 1929 Wall Street crash the beginning of the Great Depression or in the breaching of the Berlin Wall the end of the Cold War, so should it see in the election of the Thatcher government, as James Callaghan even at the time discerned, the beginning of the neo-liberal era.

During the next thirty years the economic liberals' vision crystallised into an ideology or secular religion that was eventually christened either neo-liberalism or, less kindly, market fundamentalism. With only slight exaggeration, the political economist Andrew Gamble has called neo-liberalism our era's "dominant common sense." Although it is true that the faith was stronger in some Western countries than in others, and also true that it was to some extent coloured or modified by the national political cultures with which it was mixed, everywhere it had certain basic tenets.

An ideal-typical account of the free-market faith goes, roughly speaking, like this.

According to neo-liberalism, national prosperity and growth were only able to be achieved by the actions of individuals pursuing their self-interest within free markets, through the process Adam Smith had called the operation of "the invisible hand." Similarly, global growth and prosperity could only be achieved by nations trading freely with each other on the basis of their "comparative advantage" without any form of protectionist impediment. At the heart of the neo-liberal faith was the understanding that the market order relied on competition. Competition was necessary if the vital information on which a market system depended – price signals – was to be generated. For this reason, the vested interests or rent-seekers, which undermined the operation of the free market, needed to be tamed. Monopolies had to be prevented from forming because they could set their own prices. Cartels had to be destroyed because they could set prices through collusion. Above all, trade unions had to be subdued because they interfered with the most fundamental price of all – the price of labour – and because their collective power threatened economic ruin through inflation.

In the operation of a market order, according to neo-liberal ideology, the role the state should play was strictly limited. Strong states were required but only to defend property rights and create the framework of commercial law. Beyond that, in the realm of the economy, there was not much work for states to do. According to neo-liberal ideology, most state interventions in the economy did harm. So did most government regulations. Admittedly some problems might arise from economic activity, like environmental degradation, but market failures of this kind were generally speaking of only marginal importance. And often even they were best solved not by state action but by the use of market mechanisms. Because business was more efficient than government, states should relinquish their control over the nationalised commanding heights of the economy, such as transport or energy. This process came to be known as privatisation.

Because markets were self-correcting, according to neo-liberal ideology even heavily regulated parts of the economy, like the financial sector, should be deregulated.

In philosophical terms, the fundamental value of those who shared the neo-liberal faith was freedom. Unfortunately, however, neo-liberals argued, many political thinkers had been seduced by the other great value unleashed by the French Revolution – equality. The only kind of equality not inimical to a market society was equality of opportunity. Its most important expression was equality before the law. All other attempts to advance the cause of equality in human affairs had to be resisted. At its worst, this attempt had led to the nightmare known as socialism, whose ugly potential was first revealed in Soviet totalitarianism. But a more moderate version of the idea of equality, often expressed as the quest for social justice, has also done very great harm. In trying to create a society not of absolute but relative equality, after World War II, elaborate welfare states had been created. These welfare states were also the enemies of freedom. They required citizens to pay unacceptably high levels of taxation and therefore robbed them of what was rightly theirs. Even those who received benefits from the welfare state were in danger of being reduced as a result to a debilitating condition of underclass dependency. While it was admitted that no civilised society could allow its citizens to starve to death or die of disease untreated, this minimal level of welfare assistance could be provided outside the market order without the need for the kind of elaborate welfare state created throughout the Western world during the age of the Keynesian social-democratic consensus. For all these reasons, according to the neo-liberal faith, welfare states should be at least partially dismantled. The high taxes and big government associated with the Keynesian consensus should be rejected. Any new redistributionist attempts to interfere with the rights of the wealthy, who had succeeded through their own actions in the market, had to be resisted. The quest for social justice was not merely endangering freedom. It was driven by envy, the most base of all the human passions.

The neo-liberal faith to some degree affected all Western and many non-Western countries. But its influence was felt most strongly in the Anglo-sphere – the United States, Great Britain, Australia and New Zealand. I have decided in this essay to limit my assessment of the impact of neo-liberalism to one country: the United States. The United States is by every measure the world's largest economy. Of all countries in the world, the impact of neo-liberalism was felt most purely there. All political ideologies in the end are evaluated according to their consequences. And often the impact of an ideology in the life of a particular country provides the crucial test. Just as communism was judged by what occurred inside the Soviet Union between 1917 and 1991; just as social democracy is often judged by what has occurred in Sweden since the 1930s – so will neo-liberalism be judged by what it brought to the United States from the late 1970s until today.

One thing that neo-liberalism brought the United States was a greater degree of social inequality than advanced democratic capitalism has ever before seen. Between the mid-1970s and 2006 the gross domestic product of the United States trebled; the level of labour productivity almost doubled; the Dow Jones Index rose from 1000 to 13,000. Yet astonishingly enough, during that entire period, according to several studies, the income of the average American worker and family essentially remained stagnant. This stands in very marked contrast to the preceding period of the Keynesian consensus, when the income of average working people in America increased by 2.5 to 3 per cent each year, roughly in line with the general rate of economic growth. Around 1980 the wages of ordinary workers were decoupled from gains in productivity. The long story of growing equality in the United States that had begun in the 1930s, that economic historians had christened the Great Compression, was now very dramatically reversed. The most startling statistical account of the process Joseph Stiglitz has called the new era of "trickle-up economics" is to be found in a couple of pages of a recent book, The Two Trillion Dollar Meltdown, by the by no means left-wing banker Charles Morris. From

1980 to 2006, Morris tells us, the wealthiest 10 per cent of Americans increased their share of national income from 35 per cent to 49 per cent. But what was much more remarkable, as he goes on to point out, was that almost all the action occurred at the very top of the social tree. By 2006 the wealthiest 1 per cent earned 20 per cent of national income. This represented a return to the position of 1929. Of this, the wealthiest 0.1 per cent earned 9 per cent and the wealthiest 0.01 per cent, 3.8 per cent.

To put some flesh on this statistical skeleton we can turn to some of the astonishing figures contained in Robert Reich's *Supercapitalism*. During the era of the Keynesian consensus, American CEOs earned about twenty-five to thirty times the income of their workers. On the eve of the Great Recession, they earned 300 to 500 times their salary, incomparably more than their French or German or Japanese equivalents. One of the best-paid CEOs ran Walmart. He received 900 times the income of his workers, thus earning more each fortnight than they would earn in their lifetime. By now a top investment banker took home in salary, bonuses and stock options $20–$25 million a year; a top financial trader took home some $40–$50 million. By the standards of the tiny hedge-fund-managing elite they were, however, paupers. George Soros paid himself $840 million; James Simons a cool $1.5 billion. A similar story emerges if one looks not at what the super-rich earned but at what they owned. In the 1970s, the richest 1 per cent of Americans owned 20 per cent of America. On the eve of the Great Recession, they owned some 40 per cent. By this time Bill Gates was worth $46 billion; Warren Buffet $44 billion. With wealth amounting to $90 billion, the Walmart family was by now worth almost as much as the bottom 40 per cent of Americans. I cannot resist one final figure, although it takes us beyond the United States. A decade before the Great Recession, the three richest human beings on earth owned as much as the poorest 600 million.

When George Orwell tried to give an account of the kind of society he hoped to live in, one of his stipulations was that no one should be allowed to earn more than ten times the salary of anyone else. Orwell, unfortunately, never turned his mind to how this outcome might be achieved without the assistance of the kind of monster state he warned about in *Nineteen Eighty-Four*. Orwell's kind of socialist thinking appalled the most important neo-liberal of our era, Friedrich Hayek, who saw in it the road to serfdom. In one of his last works, *Law, Legislation and Liberty*, Hayek wrote: "I have come to feel that the greatest service I can still render to my fellow men would be that I could make the speakers and writers among them thoroughly ashamed ever again to employ the term 'social justice.'" The faith in the beneficence of market outcomes shown by Hayek and other neo-liberals like him has helped blind us to the moral wrong of the situation of extreme inequality in the United States and elsewhere that has emerged over the past three decades.

Neo-liberalism in the United States coincided not only with extraordinary concentration of income and wealth. It also coincided with the rise of financial activity as the source of both, a striking process that has been christened "financialisation." Once again, a few statistics are necessary to tell the tale. In the Keynesian era, less than 20 per cent of US corporate profit came from the financial sector. By 2007 almost 40 per cent did. In the Keynesian era, US salaries in the financial and the non-financial sectors were more or less equal. By 2007 people earned in the financial sector almost double what they earned elsewhere. In 1970 Goldman Sachs employed 1300 people and in late 2008, 30,000. Although the financial sector by 2007 accounted for only 14 per cent of American GDP and 5 per cent of private-sector jobs, it accounted for almost a quarter of the value of the US stock market. At the end of the Keynesian era, it had accounted for about 6 per cent. The financialisation of the US economy received the blessing and the boosting of the neo-liberal elite. This, after all, was what the invisible hand of the free market had produced. By contrast, there can be little room for doubt that if he had lived to witness the rise and rise of finance, Keynes would have been puzzled and appalled. "The position is serious," he once wrote, "when enterprise becomes the bubble on a whirlpool of speculation. When the capital development of a country becomes the by-product of the activities of a casino, the job is likely to be ill-done."

In the decade before the arrival of the Great Recession, the most dynamic element in the US financial sector was the market in so-called "derivatives," those financial instruments whose value derives from something else, such as a bond or a stock, and which involve a gamble by a buyer and a seller on the question of their future worth. In the early 1990s the size of the derivatives market was modest. After the invention of credit derivatives in the mid-1990s – most importantly interest-rate swaps and credit-default swaps – it exploded. Around the turn of the century, derivatives contracts registered by the Bank of International Settlements already amounted to $100 trillion. On the eve of the Great Recession, the contracts were valued at more than $650 trillion. $650 trillion is more than forty times the size of the annual gross domestic product of the United States.

The derivatives market was essentially unregulated. In 1994, as Gillian Tett has shown in her outstanding study of J.P. Morgan and the derivatives industry, Fool's Gold, after a considerable amount of money had been lost by the trade in derivatives, four bills seeking regulation were sent to Congress. The derivatives industry was alarmed. It created a powerful lobby group. Not long after, the four bills were withdrawn. Clinton's treasury secretary offered the market in derivatives his blessing. In 1998, another attempt to regulate the derivatives trade was made, this time by the head of the small Commodity Futures Trading Commission, Brooksley Born. Once again, the ambition caused a panic. On this occasion the treasury secretary, Robert Rubin, his deputy Larry Summers and the head of the Federal Reserve, Alan Greenspan, intervened. They thought Born incapable of understanding finance. They believed that derivatives were the market's way of spreading risk. Born was defeated. Legislation was passed that declared a moratorium on derivatives regulation. Shortly after, she resigned her post. At much the same time, a $300 million financial-sector lobbying campaign led to the repeal of the *Glass-Steagall Act*, which had passed Congress in 1933, in the days of Roosevelt and the Great Depression, and which had created a wall between the activities of commercial and investment banks. Although the argument is disputed, some of the most influential economists and financial players regard this as a crucial change. Shortly before the crash, the CEO of Goldman Sachs, Lloyd Blankfein, expressed his deep satisfaction with the repeal of *Glass-Steagall*. Banks were now doing, he argued, what they had done in "their heyday," at the time of J.P. Morgan and the Rothschilds. "What caused an aberration was the *Glass-Steagall Act*." After the crash occurred, Joseph Stiglitz argued that the repeal had transformed the fundamentals of US banking culture for the worse. One thing at least is uncontroversial: from now on leading US banks like the Bank of America and Citigroup, as well as leading brokerages like Goldman Sachs, J.P. Morgan Chase, Lehman Brothers, Merrill Lynch and Bear Stearns, and the major hedge funds, threw themselves into the burgeoning derivatives trade.

In the late 1990s two further developments of great significance took place. In 1997 the team at J.P. Morgan developed a complex derivatives instrument known as BISTRO. This instrument allowed investment banks to insure themselves against default among their corporate loans. As the problem of loan default was at the heart of the banking business, BISTRO was a potentially revolutionary development in its history. One of the team who worked on it likened it to the Manhattan Project. The metaphor was more apt than he realised. Not long after, these instruments became known as Collateralised Debt Obligations or CDOs. CDOs were divided into tranches – junior, mezzanine and senior – depending on the level of risk. Junior tranches were highest risk. Those who purchased them earned more. Senior tranches were regarded as entirely safe. They earned less. Parts of the corporate loans converted into CDOs were uninsured. These parts were regarded as safer than safe. They were eventually given a name: super-senior. In order to allow it to lower its capital requirements covering the corporate loans it had turned into CDOs, J.P. Morgan convinced the London financial arm of America's largest insurance company, AIG, to insure the super-senior tranche through a credit-default swap. AIG Financial Services must have thought it was earning free money. As it happened, not only were they wrong; the question of the kind of insurance offered for the "safer than safe" super-senior component of CDOs would determine the future of the global economy.

In 1999, an even more portentous development took place. Those producing CDOs turned their gaze to the booming US housing market. For many years house mortgages had been turned into securities. These securities were now in turn transformed into CDOs. Like the corporate loans-based CDOs, the mortgage-based CDOs were also divided into tranches. A very high proportion of them were based on the most rapidly expanding part of the mortgage market, known, in a delightful euphemism, as sub-prime, where clients with no assets and insecure employment prospects were encouraged by mortgage companies to take out very expensive loans which often began with deceptive early "teaser" rates. Eventually the sub-prime mortgages were issued mainly for the purpose of satisfying the insatiable demand of Wall Street's major banks and brokerages for material they could transform into ultra-lucrative CDOs. The pace at which these CDOs were created was frenzied. In this frenzy, the cooperation of the major ratings agencies was required. Almost as a matter of course they turned BBB securities into AAA-rated CDOs. A trader who was convinced that this market was certain eventually to fail and who built his business by "shorting" these CDOs, that is to say by betting on their future failure, continually asked himself the overwhelming question: Can this really be allowed? By providing combinations of vulnerable sub-prime mortgages with AAA ratings, the key agencies turned a handy profit both for themselves and for the companies whose products they were supposedly rating. To call this a conflict of interest seems altogether too kind. In turn, these products were sold on to big investors, such as governments or pension funds, who were looking somewhere for high returns at a time when the Fed was keeping interest rates extremely low.

One of the key issues faced by the banks and brokerages in the creation of these CDOs was the problem of deciding the number to be used for the statistical correlation of a likely general default of the different mortgages in the CDO bundle. The information used to assess the mortgage-based CDOs all came from the time of the housing-market boom. The banks and brokerages decided to use the same modest correlation number that they used for deciding the likelihood of a general default among the individual components of their corporate loan-based CDOs. This turned out to be a serious mistake. Mathematics seemed to show a generalised default on sub-prime mortgages was virtually impossible. The mathematics was, however, based on systematically misleading data. This was not a minor matter. As with the CDOs based on corporate loans, mortgage-based CDOs also had a super-senior component. An astonishing amount of the super-senior risk was insured with credit-default swaps issued by AIG Financial Services. By 2008 it had liabilities amounting to $560 billion. This was three times more than its parent company, the world's biggest insurer, was worth. Other parts of the super-senior liabilities were either on the books of the banks dealing in CDOs or had been sold on, as supposed free money, to other banks. If the sub-prime mortgage market was ever to suffer a general collapse large enough to reach the super-senior pool, all the banks and brokerages, in the US and abroad, which were now massively involved in the trade in mortgage-based CDOs, would be in desperate trouble. So would the world economy.

In 2007 the housing bubble began to burst. Vast numbers of sub-prime mortgages defaulted. Wall Street was indeed in trouble. In March 2008, Bear Stearns was effectively bankrupt. It was bought for a song by J.P. Morgan Chase. In September 2008, the final crisis came. The massive semi-public mortgage businesses, Fannie Mae and Freddie Mac, were effectively nationalised. More fatefully, Lehman Brothers was allowed to fail. In the United States and beyond, the financial markets now froze in fear. Not only the giants of Wall Street but also many of the largest banks outside the United States, such as Deutsche Bank or USB of Switzerland or the Royal Bank of Scotland, were up to their necks in the derivatives trade. The banks were no longer willing to lend to each other. They knew too much about each other's business. The Bush administration asked Congress for US$700 billion to buy up the "toxic assets" of the banks and brokerages regarded as too big to fail. AIG was now bailed out with an initial $85 billion Federal Reserve loan. Its collapse would have taken a large part of the world's economy with it. The British government injected £25 billion into its banking system. The Irish government guaranteed all its banks' deposits. Iceland nationalised all its banks. The mad trade in derivatives, which had earned massive fortunes for the Wall Street Masters of the Universe, had by now brought the world economy to its knees.

The market faith that was at the heart of neo-liberalism was deeply implicated in this collapse. Two outstanding recent books make this clear. Gillian Tett in *Fool's Gold* has shown that many of those responsible for the architecture of the most complicated financial instruments were fervent disciples of Hayek. "If there was one thing," she argues, "that united swaps traders … it was the belief in the efficiency, and superiority, of free markets." By a different route, Justin Fox in *The Myth of the Rational Market* has shown that, on the eve of the derivatives meltdown, abstruse academic theories about the perfect rationality of the market had turned into an ideology that infected the thinking of both Wall Street traders and the US financial elite. Fox describes the ideology like this: "Financial markets knew best. They moved capital from those who had it to those who needed it. They spread risk. They gathered and dispersed information. They regulated global economic affairs with a swiftness and decisiveness that governments couldn't match." From time to time, practical men of affairs had warned about the dangers of derivatives. Allan Taylor of the Royal Bank of Canada called derivatives "a time bomb." The financier Felix Rohatyn called them "financial hydrogen bombs, built on personal computers by 26-year-olds with MBAs." Most famously, in his Berkshire

Hathaway Report of 2002, Warren Buffet argued that "derivatives are financial weapons of mass destruction, carrying dangers that, while now latent, are potentially lethal." As we have seen, members of Congress or administrators like Brooksley Born had argued the case for derivatives-market regulation. But time and again the warnings of the Cassandras had been rebuffed by finance-industry lobbyists and by neo-liberal true believers.

Undoubtedly the most important individual example here was the head of the Federal Reserve, Alan Greenspan. Consistently from the mid-1990s to 2008, Greenspan defended derivatives. Greenspan led the charge against Brooksley Born. Greenspan favoured the repeal of the *Glass-Steagall Act*. And Greenspan had time and time again offered a defence of the trade in derivatives on classic free-market Hayekian grounds. On one occasion he argued: "I believe that the general growth in large institutions has occurred in the context of an underlying structure of markets in which many of the larger risks are dramatically – I should say – fully hedged." And on another: "What we have found over the years in the marketplace is that derivatives have been an extraordinarily useful vehicle to transfer risk from those who shouldn't be taking it to those who are willing to and are capable of doing so." According to Alan Blinder, a fellow member of the Board of the Federal Reserve, "proposals to bring even minimal regulation [to the derivatives trade] were basically rebuffed by Greenspan." Blinder described Greenspan as "consistently cheerleading on derivatives." In his prescient 1998 attack on free-market fundamentalism, *False Dawn*, which commented in passing on the risk of "a systemic collapse" of the global economy posed by "the practically unknowable virtual economy of financial derivatives," John Gray posed a very interesting question: "What cataclysm in the market will it take to convince Greenspan that a new era of stable growth is merely another myth?" We now know the answer to that question. With admirable honesty, Greenspan confessed in written testimony to Congress in October 2008 that the derivatives implosion had left him in a state of "shocked disbelief." During oral testimony, Henry

Waxman asked him if his lifelong ideology had been shaken. With characteristic circumlocution, Greenspan replied: "I think I have found a flaw in the model that I perceived as the critically functioning structure that defines how the world works." What he meant by this was "Yes."

Historians are experts in predicting the past. They are not so skilled at predicting the future. Nonetheless I think there are several good reasons for believing, like the prime minister, that with the derivatives disaster and the coming of the Great Recession, the age when neo-liberalism was the dominant common sense might be drawing to its end.

Neo-liberalism rested on a single leap of faith. Because markets were believed to be self-correcting, their operation did not require the intervention of governments. Following the bankruptcy of Lehman Brothers and the freezing of financial markets across the globe, virtually no one behaved as if they believed this to be true. The heads of American banks, brokerages and insurance companies now all looked to government for assistance and for leadership. It was the US treasury secretary who drew up the plans for saving the financial system and bailing out the banks and brokerages regarded as too big to fail. It was governments, across the globe, that now injected capital into the banks or guaranteed their deposits or decided that there was no alternative to at least temporary nationalisation. And it was the governments of the G20 that set about the arduous task of creating a new regulatory structure for the international financial system. In the face of crisis, the market was completely powerless. If the banks and the brokerages had been asked to rely on the invisible hand of the market to sort out the mess their involvement in the derivatives trade had created, the world economy would have passed into freefall. At the moment of truth, the idea central to the neo-liberal faith – the superiority of the invisible hand of the market to the economic intervention of government – was shown to be a myth. Almost everyone now recognised that, in different circumstances, both market forces and government actions had their place. Stiglitz summed all this up best: "Most of the individual mistakes boil down to just one: a belief that markets are self-adjusting and that the role of government should be minimal ... The embracing by America – and much of the rest of the world – of this flawed economic philosophy made it inevitable that we would eventually arrive at the place we are today." If the neo-liberal era had begun with Ronald Reagan's witticism about government being the problem and not the solution, and if it had been entrenched when Bill Clinton observed that the era of big government was over, we might think of it as coming to an end when Barack Obama argued at his inauguration that the real issue was really not whether government ought to be big or small but whether what it did actually worked.

The coming of the Great Recession also seemed to mark a sea change in the intellectual landscape. The neo-liberal era had begun with the dethroning of Keynes, whose influence over a generation was held responsible for the arrival of stagflation. Yet if one was to judge by the behaviour not merely of governments but also international institutions, it was now as if that dethronement had never taken place. Keynes had argued that the Great Depression might have been avoided if governments had responded in the 1930s not by trying to put their houses in order by balancing their budgets but by borrowing heavily and stimulating demand. Across the globe this is precisely what governments now did. Even the originally Keynesian International Monetary Fund, which the neo-liberals had taken possession of in the early 1980s, now suddenly seemed to revert to its origins by urging governments across the globe to embark immediately on a $6 trillion spending program. It was as if Keynes had not been killed off by the neo-liberals, as was generally believed, but had merely gone into exile and waited patiently for the kind of crisis that would allow him to make a triumphant return. With the coming of the Great Recession, the most persuasive economists were the small band of Keynesians, including the two Nobel Prize winners Joseph Stiglitz and Paul Krugman. One of this band, James K. Galbraith, now joked that since the arrival of the Great Recession he had moved from the margins to the mainstream without changing a single idea. Neo-liberal economists and publicists were still arguing, but hardly anyone was listening. The neo-liberals had gained some of their influence by convincing non-economists among the political class that they represented the collective wisdom of the most successful discipline among the social sciences – economics. Not only was this proposition doubtful, it also did little to help their cause. Virtually no economist in the mainstream had predicted the coming crash. More deeply, mainstream economists had talked with growing confidence about the end of depression or recession economics and the arrival of a new era of stable economic growth, which Ben Bernanke had christened the "Great Moderation." To put it mildly, this new era had not come to pass. Two eminent economists, George Akerlof and Robert Shiller, now published a book with the Keynesian title *Animal Spirits*, which questioned the worth of a discipline whose fundamental assumption – that humans always behave rationally and on the basis of self-interest – was so self-evidently false. And from the grave, a minor Keynesian, Hyman Minsky, who had theorised about the wild speculation and Ponzi finance that long periods of unregulated financial stability would inevitably bring, was hailed as a prophet of the present discontents.

One central normative principle of the neo-liberals is that the wealth and earnings resulting from lawful behaviour conducted in the marketplace ought not to be questioned. This principle is very widely accepted. After outlining the astonishing wealth and earnings of the American "super-rich" I described earlier in this essay, even a left-of-centre economist like Robert Reich felt compelled in 2007 to remind his readers that "the super-rich are not at fault. By and large the markets are generating these outlandish results." It is easy to see how markets are responsible for the wealth of George Soros or the Walmart family. But why we should believe that it is the impersonal logic of the market that has decided to award American CEOs several times what their European or Japanese equivalents earn, or to award bankers and brokers tens of millions of dollars in bonuses and stock options each year, or, to take a different example, to award American physicians double the salary earned by other physicians in the OECD, is far from clear to me. With the arrival of the Great Recession, questions about wealth distribution on Wall Street and beyond were finally being asked. The reason was not the revelation of the actions of über-criminals like Bernie Madoff, who stole $50 billion from his clients. Even if in its scale such behaviour is unprecedented, its type is all too familiar. The reason was rather that the eyes of the general public were finally opened to the astonishing sense of entitlement to riches beyond imagining that the most respectable of the bankers and brokers had revealed. These bankers and brokers, in America and beyond, had made incalculably vast fortunes on the basis, in part, of the generous commissions paid as a result of their involvement in the $650 trillion derivatives industry. In the year Wall Street imploded, they awarded themselves $32.6 billion in bonuses. Even after the trade collapsed, taking with it a goodly part of the world's economy, they continued to regard their bonuses as no more than their just deserts. The single most disastrous business implicated in the derivatives trade was AIG Financial Services in London. This small office was largely responsible for the collapse of its parent, AIG, which required $152 billion to bail it out. After the AIG bailout, the 400 employees of the London branch received on average a bonus of $1 million each. Its head, Joseph Cassano, who had done more than anyone else to destroy AIG, received an initial golden handshake of $34 million and was put on a consultation contract of $1 million a month. Goldman Sachs received some $13 billion of the money given by US taxpayers to AIG. In July this year, it laid aside for its employees a bonus fund of $20 billion. And in early November it was revealed that while in 2006 and 2007 Goldman Sachs was spruiking $40 billion worth of AAA-rated sub-prime mortgage bonds to institutional investors, secretly and almost certainly illegally it was placing massive bets on the likely future failure of this very category of bonds.

This kind of behaviour, implicitly at least, receives the blessing of a philosophy that regards market outcomes as morally neutral and portrays the quest for social justice as a dangerous mirage and a way-station on the road to serfdom. Moreover, it occurs in a country that has told its poorest 47 million people that the provision of basic health insurance to all its citizens is well beyond its means. The Obama administration is now struggling to introduce such a system. The battle being fought is fierce. One of the most influential members of the Republican Party, Sarah Palin, has accused Obama of planning to establish death panels to kill off elderly Americans. Another, Rush Limbaugh, has gone even further, likening Barack Obama to Adolf Hitler. Even if Limbaugh does not understand it, the academic scribbler ultimately responsible for this insane thought is Hayek. If the era of the Keynesian social-democratic consensus might be thought to have begun when a mile-long queue formed in London late in World War II of people wanting to purchase a copy of the Beveridge Report, the blueprint for the British welfare state, the introduction of a decent health-care system in the United States would, for me at least, create a fitting symbol to mark the beginning of the end of the neo-liberal era.

There is a deeper reason still why it seems reasonable to predict that the neo-liberal era will soon be over. By far the largest problem humankind now faces is catastrophic climate change. Although there is no reason in theory why neo-liberals cannot rise to the challenge, as did Margaret Thatcher, in practice there are a number of reasons why they have not.

During the last two decades the mainstream of neo-liberalism formed what might best be called a companionate ideological marriage with neo-conservatism. The influence of both streams of thought was to be found in the most important right-wing think-tanks, such as the American Enterprise Institute and the Heritage Foundation in the United States and the Centre for Independent Studies and the Institute for Public Affairs in Australia. These think-tanks were important propagators in their publications of climate-change denialism, or scepticism as it is more politely called. In one case – the American Enterprise Institute – substantial payments were offered for academic papers of a denialist kind. No less importantly, the neo-liberal, neo-conservative think-tanks provided denialism with its key pseudo-sociological rationalisation: the argument that those who believed in the threat that climate change posed to the future of the Earth were in essence members of a "politically correct" elite class whose primary motivation was indifference towards the wellbeing of "ordinary people" and hatred for the achievements of the West.

There is another reason why neo-liberalism has failed to meet the challenge of climate change. Unquestionably the two most important neo-liberal ideologues were Friedrich Hayek and Milton Friedman. Hayek's most important polemic was *The Road to Serfdom*; Friedman's *Capitalism and Freedom*. Both discuss environmental damage as a case of market failure. But for both it is such a minor issue that the discussion involves a few perfunctory lines. Even though it is true that neo-liberal economists are capable of suggesting market mechanisms, like "cap and trade," as the solution to the problem of carbon emissions, it is equally true that for neo-liberalism a case of market failure as large as catastrophic climate change, which Sir Nicholas Stern has famously called the greatest such case in the history of humankind, creates great intellectual and ideological discomfort. The affective core of neo-liberalism is, after all, market faith or market fundamentalism. For this reason, neo-liberals are ideologically pre-programmed not necessarily to deny altogether but to radically downplay the significance of market failure.

Given all this, it was no accident that the only two governments in the world that refused in principle to ratify the Kyoto Protocol were the ones whose rhetoric was most strongly influenced by neo-liberalism – the Howard government in Australia and the Bush administration in the United States – who together, as a kind of Coalition of the Unwilling, contrived to create an almost instantly still-born alternative to Kyoto, the Asia-Pacific Partnership on Clean Development and Climate. It claimed preposterously that carbon emissions could be reduced without any international treaty or agreement but entirely on the basis of voluntary national action. Yet the intellectual failure of neo-liberalism to meet the challenge of climate change can be even more comprehensive than this. One tendency of neo-liberalism has been to transfer the central principle of its thinking about economics uncritically to other spheres of life. No one has done this more egregiously than one of the most significant contemporary neo-liberals, Vaclav Klaus, the president of the Czech Republic. Not only is Klaus a climate-change sceptic. He also believes that the 1930s economic argument between Oskar Lange and Hayek, over planning versus the market, can be applied unproblematically to the contemporary question of climate change. According to him, the climate-change scientists suffer from what Hayek called the socialists' "fatal conceit." As Klaus puts it, "they believe in their own omnipotency, in knowing better than millions of rationally behaving men and women what is right and wrong." For Hayek, economic prosperity rested fundamentally on millions of individuals pursuing their self-interest. For Klaus, so does the future of the Earth. Vaclav Klaus's thought is no less insane than Rush Limbaugh's.

I believe that the era of neo-liberalism is indeed drawing to a close. Just as stagflation fatally undermined the Keynesian social-democratic consensus, so too will the combination of the Great Recession and the growing recognition of the destructive role played by neo-liberalism in inhibiting an effective response to catastrophic climate change eventually discredit the idea at the heart of neo-liberalism: the faith in the magic of the free market. This, of course, will not happen overnight. It is well to remember that there was a five-year gap between the arrival of stagflation and the election of the Thatcher government.

There are two important differences between the circumstances surrounding the end of the Keynesian era in the late 1970s and the present unravelling of neo-liberalism. When the Keynesian consensus collapsed, a party-in-waiting existed, ready to seize its chance. No equivalent anti-neo-liberal party exists today. Old-style socialism is dead. Left-of-centre neo-Keynesians are far less ideological, far more divided and far more cautious than their neo-liberal adversaries. Even more importantly, at the moment of the neo-liberal collapse, humanity confronts the diabolical problem of climate change. Those who inherit the post-neo-liberal world will be obliged not merely to strive to reconcile the hope for renewed prosperity with the quest for domestic and global social justice. They will also be obliged to reconcile both these ambitions with the gravest challenge humankind has ever faced. No one yet knows what the new era will look like or what it will eventually be called. Only one thing seems at present reasonably certain. At the end of the era of free-market faith, we will be in a far better position to turn our attention to the kinds of ethical and environmental questions which, for thirty years, neo-liberalism encouraged us to evade.

Christine Nicholls

Ludwig Wittgenstein wrote in his *Philosophical Investigations*, "A picture held us captive. And we could not get outside it, for it lay in language and language seemed to repeat it inexorably." In *Radical Hope*, Noel Pearson thinks, theorises and offers suggestions outside of the bleak picture of Australian Aboriginal education that currently holds sway. But ultimately it is in education that he places his hopes for the future: "I have hope. Our hope is dependent on education. Our hope is how serious we become about the education of our people."

As the principal of a relatively large Aboriginal school (fluctuating in the vicinity of 200-plus students) in the Tanami Desert, where I lived and worked for the best part of a decade, I too once shared the same hope. And while I still believe that education is of key importance, after many years of engagement in this area I have come to the realisation that the issues of housing, health and employment need to be equal, simultaneous and concurrent foci of government and private attention before education can bring about real and lasting change. These are by no means autonomous fields.

Until such a concerted approach is made, there will continue to be small, localised success stories in the area of education, but no broad, permanent change markedly for the better. Equally, there will always be those people whom French sociologist Pierre Bourdieu described as "*des miraculés*" or the "miraculous exceptions," those educationally highly successful children who emerge from the ranks of the working class, the underclass, the unemployed or from other materially insecure families, and who really "make it." Of this group, Noel Pearson is an example *par excellence* – perhaps the most miraculous of exceptions. And such exceptions are all the more miraculous because they serve to prove the rule. In order for large numbers, indeed a critical mass, of remote-area Aboriginal children to succeed in this fashion, housing, health and employment will need just as much urgent attention as education.

At Lajamanu School the Aboriginal and non-Aboriginal teachers mostly worked extremely hard, and the majority were highly competent. Together we were relatively successful in the education enterprise. In retrospect, however, I see that placing one's hopes in education alone is not enough. When children live in houses with thirty-plus people, they do not sleep soundly, there is nowhere to do homework, health and hygiene (physical and moral) become compromised, and if the children come to school at all in such circumstances, they are tired, listless and often hungry too. No matter how competent the teacher and no matter what whizz-bang teaching methodologies teachers might embrace, such children cannot be receptive learners. If they never or only rarely see their parents engaged in meaningful work, on whom do they model themselves? On what basis do they conceptualise their adult lives? These are simply realities.

Equally, if a significant percentage of the adults and children in any given community (even if it is a "dry community," as was the one in which I lived) suffer from kidney problems, heart disease as a result of rheumatic fever, eye problems such as trachoma, scabies, hepatitis, tuberculosis or even leprosy (which has been eradicated since the time I lived there), it is difficult for these children to put energy into learning and for their communities to give the necessary support to the educational enterprise.

Likewise, when 95 per cent of the children in the school have *otitis media*, leading to educationally significant hearing loss, then it is virtually impossible for those children to learn effectively, especially when instruction is in a foreign language. Year after year Lajamanu School was visited by teams of interstate experts who specialised in the diagnosis of hearing loss caused by *otitis media*. Up to ten people would arrive at the same time. These team members tested the hearing of every child in the school and the news, predictably, was always bad. This was, of course, a very costly exercise for the government, but *never* – not even once – was any funding put into actually fixing the problem. Eventually I wearied of this over-diagnosing, and, in desperation, wrote a submission to the Disadvantaged Schools Program and finally received modest funding to put microphones and loudspeakers into two classrooms.

Only a tiny minority of teachers in the school was trained to teach English as a Second Language (ESL). Over a period of more than a decade, only a handful of qualified ESL teachers was ever appointed to Lajamanu School, despite numerous requests. Nor, for the duration, were any qualified teachers of the deaf appointed to the school. There are no trained ESL teachers at Lajamanu School now. Inexplicably, the education department sees absolutely no need for teachers in these communities to have these vital skills as part of their educational repertoire. While English is now the mandated language of instruction for the first four hours of the day in Territory Aboriginal schools, these children are only just beginning to learn it. Children are expected to master initial literacy in a language that they do not understand – in other words, to learn a new language at the same time as acquiring literacy. Obviously, this is a "double jeopardy" situation, adding an unnecessary extra layer of complexity to their already compromised learning. Little wonder that school attendances have plummeted since the introduction of the "new" initiative.

Faced with all these major challenges, Aboriginal people also find themselves repeatedly confronted by illogical, inadequate and often ill-supervised government projects. Let me provide one example from the area of housing. In the late 1970s and into the early 1980s a builder was sent to live in Lajamanu, where he "worked" for four years, presumably on building houses for the local people. For this the man received generous government funding through the local Lajamanu Housing Association. In theory, he was also supposed to be training local men to continue building houses after he left. This did not happen.

Warlpiri people bestowed the nickname of "*Warlkanji-pardu*" upon this man. In English, this means something akin to Liar, Bullshit Artist, Big-Noter or Trickster (although the -*pardu* suffix has a slightly attenuating effect – "Dear Old Bullshitter" probably hits the mark). The man, big-talking but excessively lazy, had been employed by the Lajamanu Building Association to build accommodation for the citizenry of Lajamanu, most of whom were living in humpies or outdoors at that time. His grandiose verbal schemes for single-handedly revolutionising the housing situation at Lajamanu resulted in the construction of only half a mud-brick house, which in any case partially disintegrated while he was in the process of building it. Despite the waste of thousands of dollars of public money that had been allocated to ameliorate the parlous housing situation at Lajamanu, there were no repercussions whatsoever from the government or any other watchdog. Community members were clearly aghast, but their complaints were uniformly ignored or cast aside by authorities to whom they complained. Ironically, the man was fond of boasting to his mates that he had been "given a Warlpiri name," under the misapprehension that this Warlpiri moniker was evidence of his high standing in the eyes of the Warlpiri.

Government after government has raised expectations, dashed hopes and broken promises in situations akin to this one. Lest readers think that such episodes belong to the past, one need look no further than the current government's multi-million-dollar disaster, the Strategic Indigenous Housing and

Infrastructure Program (SIHIP), in which the actual building of houses has been endlessly deferred. In stating this I am not blaming the present government alone, but drawing attention to the ongoing failure of successive governments in this area.

Earlier this year, Yirrkala School, in remote north-east Arnhem Land, was in the second round of stimulus funding to build a greatly desired language centre, but the Rudd government pulled the pin on the project, preferring, it seems, to allocate more buildings to city schools. In addition, despite Yirrkala being a nominated "growth town" and a site for education-hub development, it appears unlikely to benefit from the new National Partnership funding. In the two separate streams of funding that it has been allotted, it will receive $214,000 over 2010–11. Coincidentally, perhaps, DET is allocating this to cover salaries of cultural advisor positions. These were established in 2007 as part of the Remote Learning Partnership Agreement. So, basically, there is no extra money on which to base new programs aimed at "closing the gap." It seems that the first gap that needs to be closed is the gap between what governments say they will do, and what they actually do.

In this I am not singling out the current federal government, but making a general comment about all Australian governments. When it comes to Aboriginal affairs, each successive government, regardless of party affiliation, seems to glide into office with a Messiah complex. Each one seems to want to go down in history as the one who "fixed the Aboriginal problem." And in turn, each one fails, despite small, isolated pockets of success. This is not to say that all schemes and initiatives have been abject failures, but it is necessary to build on those small pockets of success. When governments repeatedly break agreements with Aboriginal people or refuse to take responsibility in terms of monitoring their own initiatives, this has a corrosive effect on communities and affects education, too.

If there were ever a case for bipartisan support on any issue affecting this nation, surely it is here, in the interrelated areas of Aboriginal education, health, housing and employment. While often politicians hold that their differences are major ideological ones, this is frequently not so. Rather, more often than not it is a matter of political grandstanding – if the previous government endorsed a particular project, method or approach, the current one won't, simply on principle. And so the depressing cycles of failure and disappointment repeat themselves, because effective measures are irrationally discontinued.

So while I agree that education is of utmost importance, it is hard to envisage long-term qualitative improvement in education without equal attention to health, housing and employment. Only then will it really become possible to implement a No Excuses framework – a highly desirable goal, but, unfortunately, probably not fully achievable at the present time.

Noel Pearson is spot-on when he writes that governments and their bureaucracies (and, by implication, others in the field of Aboriginal education) have no cultural memory. This applies, *par excellence*, to the field of Aboriginal education. While Pearson alludes to policy *failure*, educational successes are just as easily forgotten, and some policies are not given sufficient time nor enough governmental or systemic support to have any real chance of succeeding.

Bilingual education, for example, was constantly undermined by the Northern Territory education department in a range of ways, despite strong endorsement and support from Aboriginal communities and – albeit limited, for reasons that should be clear from this response – evidence of success. The greatest furphy about Aboriginal-language programs in schools is that they involve orality and literacy *exclusively* in Indigenous languages. In fact, in the majority of cases these programs were seriously subverted by the education department's failure to provide English as a Second Language (ESL) teachers to the Territory's Aboriginal schools. Virtually all of the Aboriginal schools in remote parts of the Territory are in fact bilingual – this is the daily on-the-ground reality – whether or not it is official policy. Therefore, whether or not official bilingual education programs are in place, children in these schools merit qualified teachers to teach them English. Since newly arrived migrant children receive such consideration, it is scandalous that Aboriginal children whose first language is not English do not.

In addition, a quality document is urgently needed for prospective ESL teachers working with Aboriginal students whose first language is not English, identifying the particular areas of difficulty the children encounter when learning English. To give just one example, at Lajamanu, where I worked, Warlpiri children had difficulty learning the correct use of both the definite and indefinite articles, because there are no articles in Warlpiri. Therefore ESL teachers need to teach directly to this area of difficulty. This is not to imply any kind of deficit; there are no articles in Japanese either, and sometimes even the most sophisticated and fluent Japanese speakers and writers of English experience continuing difficulty in mastering the use of English articles.

Furthermore, Aboriginal education in remote Australia is not entirely dysfunctional (an impression one might gain by reading Pearson's essay). Unfortunately, successive governments have forgotten the success stories just as much as they have airbrushed over their own policy failures. The latter becomes evident because these failures are recycled at regular intervals, in the guise of new schemes or initiatives. (I have observed at least three such cycles now.) There are curriculum and other education-related initiatives that have worked resoundingly well, and these need to be documented and published for use by prospective teachers in Aboriginal schools. Gathering and publishing stories of "best practice" in Aboriginal education is a matter of urgency, especially because of this endemic problem of faulty institutional memory syndrome.

I will provide one example from my own experience. After I had lived and worked at Lajamanu for at least five years, the Aboriginal and non-Aboriginal teachers in the school decided that everyone in the community would benefit from a clearly articulated school policy. To this end we organised a pupil-free day and invited every adult member of the community to contribute to the policy-formation process. A highly regarded senior educator working at the University of Western Sydney was asked to convene the process, to ensure, *inter alia*, neutrality. Many people turned up on the appointed day, including Aboriginal and non-Aboriginal community members, very old Warlpiri people, young Warlpiri people, the local Christian minister, missionaries, nurses and the plumber. The process of obtaining people's views was a fair one and people could speak in whatever language they wished – either Warlpiri or English. Interpreters were at hand for the monolinguals present. The entire day was recorded in order for there to be clarity about the issues on which consensus had been achieved. It took all day and many issues were thrashed out. The result was a policy document that gave me, as the school principal, a clear mandate to act in certain sensitive areas on which I had previously wished to act, but had met with resistance from certain powerful individuals in the community. Among these was the vitally important question of school attendance, which was strongly supported by everyone who attended the policy day. As a result, I could confidently begin work on improving school attendance, which at that point was sitting at about 65 per cent to 70 per cent.

After this, the local Aboriginal police aide, a senior man in the community, served, on my behalf, "Intention to Prosecute" notices to parents who repeatedly failed to send their children to school. Although the measure did not always proceed without a hitch, Lajamanu's school attendance soared to the highest in all Aboriginal schools in the Northern Territory, by 1989 hovering between 90 per cent and 97 per cent. This was more than comparable with that of non-Indigenous schools in the Territory. By that time, most absenteeism was explained by illness rather than truancy. As a result of this measure, one boy who continued to resist attending school with what seemed to be the constant excuse of "I'm feeling sick today" was consequently examined by the local health clinic. It was found that he had serious kidney disease. Thus this action probably saved his life.

The point about this story is that addressing the problem of habitual school truancy had (more or less) full community support, and could not have been achieved without it. The school also garnered community support because of the large number of Aboriginal trainee teachers working in it to deliver the bilingual program. Many Aboriginal people feel more comfortable in delivering their children into the hands of their own people, rather than non-Aboriginal teachers about whom they know little or nothing, unless they stay for lengthy periods.

This leads to one concern that I feel I must express about Pearson's essay: his lack of focus on the need for adult Aboriginal presence in schooling. I believe this to be essential for success in Aboriginal education, where the preconceptions of teachers often differ markedly from those they are teaching. Some of the current approaches to and orthodoxies about Aboriginal education run dangerously close to interfering with or even usurping the normal parenting process, and border on treating all Aboriginal parents and extended family members as if they are, *ipso facto*, dysfunctional. This is not so and if this (largely unspoken) policy direction continues, the effect will be disastrous.

The "lap-reading" program at Lajamanu School was one means of including Aboriginal adults in the school. Each morning, first thing, mothers would come along to the preschool, transition and grades one and two classrooms, and read books to their children in either Warlpiri or English. It is essential that Aboriginal adults become part of their children's education, not just in some flaky "parents as partners" mode, which has turned into a meaningless mantra, but in ways that actually take older family members into classrooms to play a meaningful role. Such programs also allow families to learn what actually takes place inside those classrooms. It is not enough for Aboriginal children to have Aboriginal teachers, although it would also be a great advantage if more could be done to recruit young Aboriginal students into tertiary programs in the field of education.

The late Eric Willmot, an Aboriginal man and former director-general of education in South Australia, suggested that Aboriginal children frequently acquire what he described as "technical literacy" at school, but do not take on board the "culture of literacy." This is why many of these kids, even when they have been taught by methodology that includes phonics (as were the children at Lajamanu School), never actually become readers. In cultures where the intergenerational transmission of knowledge is predominantly by word of mouth, children need exposure to real books if they are to become readers. In the 1980s, with a few exceptions, there wasn't a single book in any Warlpiri home at Lajamanu. Incidentally but significantly, in the very successful lap-reading program, in many instances the mothers' own literacy levels soared, because they were reading to their children on a daily basis. Importantly, too, those mostly very young mothers were acting as role models for their children, just as Noel Pearson's own father had for his son by demonstrating his love of books, particularly the Bible.

Of course, phonics has an important place in the early literacy education of all young children, because they do need word-attack skills and they do need to know how to sound out words. I don't know of any teachers who would deny that, and I don't think that this area is as ideology-riven as Pearson would have us think. It seems to be more of an issue among politicians, academics and shock-jocks than it is among classroom teachers. But on its own phonics (and any other strategy for beginning readers) is not enough. No single approach to teaching literacy is enough, in isolation.

Encountering real books – that is, literature, not just commercial reading schemes that deliver scripted and frequently convoluted texts to provide opportunities for "pattern practice" – needs to be part of the equation. If children do not develop a love of books and literature, notwithstanding their mastery of the so-called "basic skills" of phonics and sounding out, they are destined to become functioning a-literates. That is, they will be able to function at a very basic level of deciphering individual words, filling in forms etc., but never develop that real love of reading that will lead them towards tertiary education and beyond. In this respect Pearson's basing his faith on one particular commercial reading scheme is simplistic and naive. Besides, the particular scheme that he endorses has real shortcomings, although that is beyond the scope of this response. Direct Instruction (or DISTAR) will certainly teach children to "bark at print," but that is not literacy in any fundamental sense. Direct Instruction, which has been marketed aggressively and effectively, has had limited success in inculcating word-attack skills, but more often than not that is because it's the first time ever that the child has been the recipient of one-on-one or small-group teacher instruction. I would reiterate that I am an advocate of phonics-based instruction for beginning readers, so long as it is one part of the teacher's arsenal, not the only strategy – because it can take a child only so far.

It seems that Pearson is unwittingly projecting a very narrow conceptualisation of what constitutes literacy in his essay. The great majority of successful teachers, including myself, utilise a range of strategies in teaching children how to read – designed to lead children into taking the next step, that of becoming literate, and "hooked on books."

There is absolutely no substitute for highly skilled, intelligent teachers. Attempts to "teacher-proof" (or even child-proof) reading instruction or any other form of instruction are nothing short of insulting to all involved and, for obvious reasons, are, in the longer term, bound to fail. Teachers need to make critically important educational decisions all the time. To resign oneself to sup-posedly teacher-proof alternatives smacks of desperation. Aboriginal children (and all children) deserve more than that.

Quality teaching cannot be disentangled from quality teachers as readily as Pearson suggests. This part of his essay is also somewhat contradictory. Earlier Pearson had acknowledged the critical significance of several inspirational teach-ers in his own early education. In addition, there was one teacher he does not remember very well, but nevertheless he describes her as being effective in a plodding way, despite being less than inspiring. He contends that this teacher was adequate, on the grounds that the learning materials she provided were sound. An alternative explanation is that the young Noel Pearson survived a year of being taught by this rather lazy-sounding teacher (we've all had one at some point) because he had already received the life-altering gift of exciting, motivat-ing teachers who took a real rather than merely passing interest in his future. Moreover, it seems that this "average" teacher did not actively perpetrate any harm with respect to the children in her care – but it has to be remembered that poor teachers can have a seriously and permanently deleterious effect on impressionable young children, regardless of the particular armoury of instruc-tional materials they use.

Substandard teachers are frequently the strongest advocates of the "culturally appropriate" curricula that Pearson so rightly scorns. Often the latter are simply an excuse for lazy teaching. Practically no teacher effort is required for teachers to set aside two and a half hours in the morning for children to write a two- or three-line "I went hunting for bush tucker on the weekend" story.

With respect to Noel Pearson's ideas about governments having a formal responsibility in terms of protection of Indigenous cultural diversity and lan-guages, I can only concur strongly, and agree that both individuals and govern-ments need to take a No Excuses approach to this, too. Indeed, Australia's remaining Aboriginal languages are in urgent need of legislative protection, otherwise soon there may be none left to protect.

However, I firmly believe that Pearson's idea of divvying up the school day into "Class" and "Culture" is not tenable. To allocate the less serious part of the day – by which time children in remote areas have become tired, bored and hot – to learning in and about their own languages and cultural heritage sends out a powerful negative message about their relative lack of importance both in the curriculum and in everyday life. Besides, language and culture are not "things" to be artificially separated or quarantined from learning generally. Nor can they be disentangled from the specific subject matter being taught, if one is committed to a serious approach.

There is a lot more that could be said in response to *Radical Hope*. Pearson deserves widespread, generous praise for rethinking the nature of contemporary Aboriginal education, and especially for aspiring to transform the lives of many disadvantaged Aboriginal children through education. Equally, his aspiration to hold on to Aboriginal knowledge and cultural practices, languages and traditions, some of which are experiencing severe strain, is of the utmost importance, as is his insistence that governments, as well as individuals, have critically important responsibilities in this respect.

Nonetheless, at times Pearson has a tendency to offer simple answers to some very complex questions. For example, it is well nigh impossible to isolate educational disadvantage from the closely connected areas of health, housing and employment; and there is no single commercial reading scheme that is capable of "doing the trick" when it comes to inculcating "cultural," as opposed to merely "technical," literacy. Nevertheless, Pearson should be commended for opening up the discussion in a way that is both urgent and necessary. If Aboriginal education cannot be conceptualised in a different way than it has been in the past, the cycle of failure will be repeated inexorably. Returning to Wittgenstein, it is vital that we do not remain captive to the cheerless picture that we have of Aboriginal education, eternally unable to get outside of it. While Pearson may not have sketched out an entirely new picture, he points to its very real possibility. I sincerely hope that Australians will rise to Noel Pearson's implicit challenge by responding to his provocative essay creatively, constructively and energetically.

Christine Nicholls

Chris Sarra

Having just read Noel Pearson's *Quarterly Essay*, I regret that he hasn't had the time to take us up on our offer to visit at least one of our Stronger Smarter schools across the country. There is so much we could help him understand. I found his analysis of my work a little misguided and somewhat naive. While he tries, he clearly struggles to get the fundamental importance of how schools must develop and embrace a positive Aboriginal identity in a schools context, and surprisingly he offers virtually nothing on developing and embracing Aboriginal leadership in education. Perhaps this is symptomatic of a legal mind too much in dialogue with consultants, as compared to an educator in dialogue with a national network of educators.

Ultimately this doesn't matter when we consider his demands. Noel wants Aboriginal children to retain and sustain a sense of pride in their cultural identity. He wants them to be stronger. He demands a No Excuses policy that is determined to deliver academic excellence for our children. He wants them to be smarter.

There is always room in our ranks for others to join in our demand for a stronger, smarter future for Indigenous Australian children. He is welcome on my team any day.

Chris Sarra

Tony Abbott

Even when he is on the other side of an argument, Noel Pearson rarely seems simplistic, partisan, self-congratulatory or ahistorical. He has lived the predicament of Aboriginal people struggling to reconcile their ways with modernity, thought about it with great sophistication, and written and spoken about it with unique power. Agree or disagree, it's hard to deny that he speaks with authority. That's why he's widely seen as a kind of modern-day prophet. Despite, for instance, concluding a thunderous 1998 oration with the call to be rid of "this putrid government," he had a much more complex view than the other, more predictably one-sided speakers on native title at that packed and roaring public meeting in Mosman. It was my first personal contact with Pearson. As the local MP, I found his attack on the then government was hardly endearing. It was pretty clear, though, even then, that Pearson understood how much more there was to Aboriginal disadvantage than simple racism.

When, a couple of years later, he began his long crusade against the unconditional welfare that was poisoning his people, members of that very government were among his most enthusiastic supporters. I was pleased, as employment minister, to have "whole of government" responsibility for commonwealth programs in Cape York because it gave me the chance to work with Pearson rather than just to agree with him. Pearson, I'm sure, already knew from bitter experience what I began to learn in that period between 2001 and 2003: namely, that it's much easier for well-intentioned governments to spend money than to make a difference. Still, over the course of several visits, including one camping trip with Pearson, Fred Chaney and some troubled Aboriginal youths from Aurukun, I came to think that perhaps the most serious obstacle to real reconciliation was modern Australians' failure to exceed the level of personal commitment to Aboriginal people that had been shown by the missionaries of former times. They had bled with them and bound their wounds. Many had left their bones in the communities they served. This generation's greater sensitivity towards Aboriginal culture has not yet translated into a more widespread inclination to spend long years performing thankless tasks in hardship posts.

Last year, Pearson arranged for me to spend three weeks as a teacher's aide in Coen. This year, it was ten days assisting the truancy team in Aurukun. In his *Quarterly Essay*, Pearson commends the MULTILIT remedial reading program denounced as "rote learning" by much of the educational establishment. When I recently returned briefly to Coen, I found pupils who had been illiterate a year earlier writing simple short stories thanks to MULTILIT. In his essay, Pearson eviscerates the academic orthodoxy which makes "culture" an excuse for Aboriginal students' under-performance and even non-participation in education. At Aurukun, thanks to the truancy team funded and organised by Pearson's Cape York Partnerships through the welfare reform process begun under the Howard government, school attendance rates have risen from about 30 per cent last year to over 60 per cent now. Of course that's still far too low and the academic results are not yet in. Undeniably, though, it's an important start.

Pearson's essay elegantly restates his now well-known positions on the importance of a standard academic education and on the need for Aboriginal people to be able to participate in the broader economy on their merits. That, though, is not his main point. Effective participation in wider society is more a by-product of the education that he wants for young Aborigines; it's not the main objective. Even in the most remote places, pre-prepared food, pay TV and four-wheel drives have had their inevitable impact. Aboriginal culture remains distinctive, but it is often but a distant echo of the high culture of traditional Aboriginal people. For understandable reasons Pearson is not very interested in preserving a contemporary Indigenous culture characterised by unemployment, substance abuse and domestic violence. He wants to restore fluency in traditional languages and the intimacy with country that can only come from traversing it on foot. In places where such a culture is no longer automatically passed on, Pearson thinks, education will be needed to create the mental aptitude and the critical mass for effective cultural transmission.

As is so often the case, just when he might have become pigeonholed, Pearson has the capacity to surprise both his backers and his critics. His call for a longer school day so that Aboriginal children can receive a sound general education is, of course, a challenge to the political Left. His bigger challenge, though, is reserved for the Right. Pearson wants the longer school day also to accommodate serious, sustained teaching in traditional Aboriginal culture: the language, lore and ritual of particular Aboriginal groups. Without an education in the "cultural hearth," as he calls it, Aboriginality may survive as an identity but it is unlikely to endure as a series of cultures. He's challenging Aborigines to become, in his words, a "serious people": like the Jews, perhaps the world's most successful minority, who have succeeded brilliantly in wider society while maintaining both their sense of identity and their distinctive beliefs and practices.

For all his consciousness of past injustice and of historical dispossession, Pearson is also an Australian. The civilisation that the British brought to this country from 1788 has ultimately benefited everyone, Aboriginal people included. Inevitably, Aboriginal people suffered grievously in the initial clash between modern and ancient cultures. Even so, British settlement brought immense changes for the better. As Pearson puts it, "the Enlightenment was not ... a European ... [but] a human illumination." This is the concession that Pearson makes to his non-Aboriginal fellow Australians. In return, the concession he seeks from them is a commitment to maintain Aboriginal cultures as living entities rather than as memories recorded in archives and artefacts stored in museums.

Although Pearson knows it won't be easy, I suspect he underestimates the magnitude of this task. The Jews are the most successful practitioners of cultural maintenance, but most Jewish people cling to the culture rather than to the religion; indeed, to liberal versions of it that might not pass Pearson's threshold test. Pearson concedes that individual Aborigines might choose to assimilate, as many Jews have over the centuries. Still, real respect for Aboriginal people, he thinks, means empowering them to keep their culture as well as to change it or to lose it, if that's their choice. Government, of course, unlike Pearson, could not be partial about the choices Aboriginal people make.

The challenge, for those who have been Pearson's philosophical fellow travellers up till now, is to accept that biculturalism, at least for Aboriginal people, is a worthy object of Australian government policy and is worth paying for. That should not be too much to ask. After all, Western civilisation, especially its English-speaking form, has never demanded of people that they acknowledge a single immutable identity. Because it is unique to our country, support for Aboriginal culture is a responsibility of Australian government in a way that support for other minority cultures clearly is not.

In his final scripted speech as prime minister, John Howard acknowledged how far he'd come in his attitudes to Aboriginal issues. Undoubtedly, his late-flowering friendship with Pearson was a key factor in his personal journey from resistance to engagement. Over the years, Pearson has prompted quite a few conservative Australians to a change of heart. He's now inviting us to go a little bit further than the former prime minister was prepared to, but it's a project that we should be ready to support.

Tony Abbott

Peter Shergold

When I was the secretary of the Department of the Prime Minister and Cabinet, one of the more sensible things that I did was to engage Noel Pearson as a consultant. In truth, although the Cape York Institute for Policy and Leadership delivered a respectable report, the contractual relationship was not a great success. Pearson had too many things on the go and his formidably broad shoulders carried an increasing burden of responsibilities. No wonder that even then, beneath the hopefulness of his message, he was "prone to bouts of doubt and sadness."

For me, though, the appointment was important. Pearson was engaged as an adviser on social policy, not as an expert on Aboriginal affairs. It reflected my growing recognition that on the underlying themes of his challenging essay – the meaning of community, the complex balance of personal and state responsibility, the tragedy of learned helplessness and "social-order deficit" – Pearson had bold ideas which could significantly improve our understanding of welfare reform.

The consultancy was also a means to open a dialogue with the prime minister, John Howard, which helped to reframe the government's thinking. What Pearson offered was precisely what he attributes to Steven Wilson, the chief of the Ascend Charter School in New York: he had come to a position which could and "should not be pigeonholed to the political Right or the Left."

When I persuaded Pearson that his voice might have greater political influence, I'd already spent fifteen years honing my own administrative ineptitudes in Indigenous affairs. I'd served in the Aboriginal and Torres Strait Islander Commission (ATSIC) for three and a half years and, later, as secretary of the departments of employment and then education. In those roles I had pushed for more effective programs to bridge the appalling chasm of disadvantage faced by so many Indigenous people. I'd exercised bureaucratic control with purpose and commitment. I'd genuinely believed that all Australians should receive a fair chance in life and that government policies could help to achieve that goal. It sounds, even as I write it, so touchingly naive. Perhaps my faith could be characterised as "romantic indigenism."

It is clear to the most casual reader that Pearson is not an enthusiast for Australia's public services, the "creators, filers and archivists of massive piles of history." It is not, as Pearson argues, that they retain no memory of policies; indeed, the remembrance by many individual public servants of the lack of substance behind so much vainglorious political rhetoric too often feeds hard-nosed cynicism. They smile, inwardly, at each "new" and "fresh" initiative. They know, because they have seen at first hand what most Australians do not, that self-determination has too often meant Indigenous communities organising their own second-rate services in Third-World conditions. The "legions of bureaucrats [now] rebadging policy documents and programs with the new rubric" know exactly what they are being asked to do.

Public servants are not bad people. Indeed, those who work in Indigenous affairs, both black and white, usually begin with a genuine desire to make a beneficial difference. That, I'm pretty sure, was my ambition. Only with time did I come to realise that goodwill too rarely translated into the benefits that I had anticipated. By the time I ended up in the Department of the Prime Minister and Cabinet, I was already painfully aware that in public policy the very best of intentions can result in the very worst of outcomes.

I had come to recognise that the making of policy (the sexy end of the job for most senior public servants) was nothing without its effective delivery. I was frustrated at how little the real-world experience of community-level bureaucrats influenced either the design of policy or its administration. I pushed hard for whole-of-government approaches centred on the citizen. I set up a Cabinet Implementation Unit to monitor whether government programs were being delivered on time, on budget and to expectations. I gave much greater recognition to the importance of project management. I had come, from my own experience, to the point at which Pearson now finds himself confronting Groundhog Day – that policy is vacuous unless it "grapples with the challenges of implementation."

It was from listening to Noel Pearson that I came to realise that something more profound was wrong. That failure goes to the heart of his essay on educational reform (which, I'm pleased to see, gives appropriate credit to the pioneering work of the Aboriginal academic Maria Lane). His message reverberates far beyond the schoolyard.

The problem is that no matter what the government policy, the means of delivering it too often externalises responsibility. Bureaucrats – along with social workers, case managers, lawyers, teachers and doctors – use their professional power to take control. They may not think so, but they do. The language might be that of self-determination, but the reality is welfare dependence.

Pearson taught me a simple but profound truth: if you treat people as dependents, they learn dependence. They become passive. That has been the essence of Cape York's welfare-reform advocacy for the last decade. It is the point at which self-awareness and moral responsibility meet. It is the axis at which the attempts to address social exclusion become the means to reinforce it.

Putting aside any debate about the details of Pearson's preferred educational model – such as the phonics-based MULTILIT literacy education program and the Computer Culture project – the essence of his approach lies in giving individuals and communities control. Rejecting the imposed notion of culturally appropriate and socially relevant education as ideological catch-cries for an approach which limits possibilities, Pearson instead looks to a bicultural future. His radical hope is that high-quality mainstream education can go hand-in-hand with the retention and revitalisation of Aboriginal culture.

I do not know whether demarcating "Class" and "Culture" in the Cape York classrooms will provide both the basis of economic opportunity and preserve the homeland of the soul. I can see both sides of the argument between Pearson and Dr Chris Sarra, but, in truth, I see their equally strong advocacy of No Excuses education as of greater significance than their differences. Others can debate these polemics. I have been only an "educrat" and an academic, and neither career, in my experience, offers much in the way of educational theory or the methodology of teaching.

What interests me most in Pearson's essay is the increasing intensity of his aversion to the progressives who "impede the prospects of the disadvantaged for whom they profess empathy and solidarity." Public servants – generally well-educated and well-motivated people – are part of that elite. Too often they, and many of the community advocacy organisations who work with governments, undermine the ability of individuals and communities to exert control over their own lives.

By the act of delivering government policies, program administrators often undermine self-reliance. Too rarely is self-interest, the ability to tailor government services to one's own needs, given licence – certainly not to those who are most disadvantaged and in greatest need of support. In Pearson's language, Indigenous Australians are victimised but they do not need to be victims. They are made so, in part by the way in which too many government programs and services are delivered as "sit-down" money.

Pearson's radical hope of educational reform will not be fulfilled unless the Aboriginal people of the Cape York Peninsula can take progressively greater control of their own lives. Whether they are seeking economic opportunity, living with a long-term health condition or struggling with a disability (or, indeed, all three), they need to be given greater opportunity to improve their lives by directing government support to their own needs. With that comes the requirement to recognise that their entitlements come with obligations, not least to live up to their responsibilities as parents. The local school communities require concomitant authority to continue to pursue their own approaches to educational philosophy, curriculum and governance. Individuals and communities need to be recognised as collaborators in the design and delivery of government policy.

These goals, to my mind, are not specific to Cape York. They apply not only to Aboriginal people and Torres Strait Islanders. They are not confined to the "education revolution." They are the essence of a more profound transformation in the way in which Australia seeks to create an inclusive and engaged society. Noel Pearson's message that the success of government policy will be determined by the mode of its implementation should become the catechism of public service. Perhaps that is too radical a hope?

Peter Shergold

Peter Sutton

There will likely be many technical disagreements over Noel Pearson's views on pedagogy. That subject is not mine, nor is it the focus here. Instead I will use this small space to try to understand the relationship between his critique of 1970s-style liberationist ideology and its remaining adherents, and the extraordinary levels of emotional heat being directed against Pearson and others who have mounted parallel criticisms in recent times.

Pearson's latest raid on Left-liberal orthodoxies will probably yield him a new crop of enemies, a fresh layer of angry educational people this time, to be added to those still reeling from his disembowelment of welfarist and segregationist models of social wellbeing for his people. As usual they can be expected to be among those who have found themselves no longer progressive and marginally placed critics of the established order, but old young people now embarrassedly holding more power than they ever dreamt of. Pearson's argument is that, as so often, some of the self-perceived liberalisations imposed by parts of this elite actually result in disenfranchisement of those most in need of compensatory assistance in life. After post-colonial embarrassment, we now have the potential for much post-post-colonial self-dismay.

In the context of an assault on "critical literacy," for example, Pearson analyses the "leftist" push for drumming up critique and creativity in young minds, while downgrading truly liberating skills such as the power to read. He describes it as the inculcation of a certain ideological outlook through the teaching of politically correct manners. It is the "the teaching of false consciousness, powered by moral vanity." Paulo Freire's once messianic afterglow as a '70s liberationist educationalogue is reclassified by Pearson as his "baleful legacy."

Such cattle-prod language was bound to get Pearson into trouble with those most deeply wedded to the positions and values he wants to carve up in his negative programs. Of course he also has massive positive programs, but they do

not generate the flames of his heartily felt dumping on the Left-liberal orthodox. Similarly, his opposition to the use of race alone as a basis for self-esteem
and pride, especially when so little actual achievement of anything may be
required, must raise the hackles of those with a philosophical commitment to
ethnic self-admiration, if not also those with even merely a venal interest in
the commodification of Aboriginality as a tradeable essence. When people are
told to be proud, but are not empowered to themselves create anything of
which they can be proud, they must know, as everybody else does, that a cha-
rade is in play. That doesn't stop the show, of course. This is not surprising.
The same transparent valorisations of outwardness also fail to curtail sales of
Who magazine.

Pearson's essay covers much more than these topics, of course.

I'll propose some reasons why I think the temperature around these issues has
gone up so far so fast, and why so much of the debate is now being conducted
in *ad hominem* and *ad feminam* terms. It's true that some angry people have used
some strong language. Pearson, Marcia Langton and myself are not alone there.
If you stick your head up, someone will want to kick it, as Doug Anthony would
say. You say *moral vanity*, and I'll hit back with *moral panic*. This much can be very
schoolyard. But there is a lot more to it.

This is because the post-orthodox critique threatens more than mere opin-
ions, entrenched or otherwise. It threatens moral selves. It is a danger not just
to freedom from self-doubt, but to many people's ethical self-regard, to their
biographies, to their legacies. So many now in this position of fight or flight
were once idealistic young people who gave much of their lives, especially after
the early 1970s, to the high hopes of the principles and processes that are now,
even if only selectively, under such a cloud. This applies to people in Aboriginal
affairs, but it also applies to many other departments of Australian life. This
much of their potential for resistance may seem purely secular, purely psycho-
logical, but for many it goes further. It is often deep-seated faith. The failure of
such an idealism can be a small death of the spirit.

Like other devotional fortresses, this one doesn't rest much on empirical
evidence. This is why empirical evidence is such a weak threat to its comforts.

This idealism is the sort of faith that allows one to be a transcendental utopian
at the same time as being a materialist atheist. The first driving force in its phys-
iology is negative rather than positive; the central spring is criticism. One's
goodness is first demonstrated by the badness of others, and by one's manifest
skills in exposing it. It is not, primarily, a matter of one's character. Character is
out of style, although not with Pearson.

The cliché of "perpetual protest mode" is snug here. Protest is at times a perpetual-motion machine, feeding itself but never satisfied, a dog happily chasing its tail in anger. The film *Five Easy Pieces* (1970) comes to mind. Terry and Palm are hitchhikers in the back seat, having been picked up by Bobby (Jack Nicholson) and Rayette (Karen Black):

> TERRY: In my personal observation, I think that more people are neat than are clean ...
>
> PALM: In my personal thing, I don't see that. I'm seeing more filth. A lot of filth. What they need to do every day, no, once in a while, is a cockroach thing, where they spray the homes. And uh ... can you imagine, if their doors were painted a pretty color, and they had a pot outside, with ...
>
> TERRY: Yeah, it could be adorable ...
>
> PALM: And they picked up! I mean, it wouldn't be filthy, with Coke bottles and whiskey, and those signs everywhere ...
>
> *She gestures angrily out the window at the roadside billboards.*
>
> PALM (CONT'D): ... they oughta be erased! All those signs, selling crap, and more crap, and, I don't know, it's disgusting, I don't even want to talk about it!
>
> BOBBY: Well ...
>
> PALM: It's just filthy. People are dirty. I think that's the biggest thing that's wrong with people. I think they wouldn't be as violent if they were clean, because then they wouldn't have anybody to pick on ... Oofh ... Dirt ...
>
> RAYETTE: Well ...
>
> PALM: Not dirt. See, dirt isn't bad. It's filth. Filth is bad. That's what starts maggots and riots ...

Utopian and negativist at the same time, the '70s dreamer and freedom-fighter often preferred to be agin the government, not part of it. But middle-aged Boomery and the inexorability of the mortgage have brought a rise up the political and bureaucratic and academic food chains, the chance to do things, and thus the overweening threat of facing reality. Success has created an unprecedented opportunity for the experience of failure. No wonder collars are hot.

Some of us have had to learn bitterly that it can be better to go softly-softly when trying not to lose an audience. But for many of us, including Pearson, fidelity to wrath also comes as part of the character package. Diplomacy, needed as it is, also remains forever a form of untruth. It is hard to believe Pearson would manage to have the drive required for his positive reform offensive without the foil of opposition.

Yet this is an opposition whose anger, at first slow to wake up and get stirred into action, is itself partly his own creation. That is why he has them still partly on the back foot.

Peter Sutton

Fred Chaney

I confess to experiencing moments of joy when reading Noel Pearson's essay. The opening pages made the rest of the piece irresistible reading. Like Noel, I found Lear's *Radical Hope* a beautiful book, which has remained in my thoughts. It captured for me the question that seems an urgent one for Aboriginal people: What does it mean to be Aboriginal in modern Australia? Before the culture of white settlers came to dominate, the meaning was clear. But the changes that occurred have made the old order, the old meaning, at best just one part of present Aboriginal identities. Crow chieftain Plenty Coups' statement – *"after this nothing happened"* – describing his life after the removal of the fundamental under-pinnings of Crow culture – has to be seen in the context of his ongoing life, which lasted well beyond that time and involved distinguished service to the Crow nation. Lear's book is about what he could have meant by such a statement. But it seems clear that in terms of what was and what was no more, nothing could happen: the basis of Crow culture was gone. Lear's reconstruction of Plenty Coups' reasoning following a dream is that he was told that the traditional way of life was coming to an end and that, in these circumstances, "finding a way to flourish is the task for a new generation of Crow."

This seems to capture where European settlement has left Aboriginal people. It poses a key question that only Aboriginal people can answer: What does it mean to be Noongah or Adnamathana or any of the other Aboriginal identities in 2009 and beyond?

Noel offers "for discussion" what he describes in his essay as a question vital to Aboriginal people: "what it might mean to be a serious person and what it might mean to be a serious people … when people are striving to maintain and to transmit to future generations their pre-modern cultures and languages in a modern, global world." His conclusion is that Aboriginal hope depends on how serious Aboriginal people become about the education of their people. Thus, the first eleven pages of the essay pose a challenge for Aboriginal people. Much of the next ninety pages challenges educators and others to accept their responsibilities.

No writer is more at risk of selective quotation than Noel Pearson. That makes comment on his essay difficult. Here, as with his other writing, there is a risk of cherry-picking numerous quotable lines to confirm one's own views and ideological predilections. It is worth noting his reaffirmation of points made in earlier writings: his view that racism is a terrible ongoing burden and that dispossession has an ongoing impact is often overlooked by those quoting him on welfare reform. He also repeats another view of his: to believe one can advance more than one side in a dialectical tension is an illusion. This is the one point on which I seriously disagree with Noel. The issues facing Aboriginal Australians involve consideration of the impact of welfare, but, as Noel has eloquently argued elsewhere, they also involve the recognition of rights, including rights to land, and dealing with racism. Noel's passionate advocacy of welfare reform and tackling addiction has involved leaving the rights and racism agendas to others. It is for others, presumably governments, to deal with the totality of the agenda. I think that has been a mistake and has led to a distorted national debate because of Noel's pre-eminent position in that debate. His singular capacity to present a compelling case has led to the adoption of a false premise: that there is a single silver bullet available, welfare reform. In fact, it is only one critical piece of the jigsaw rather than the whole picture. Education is another key piece.

The chapter entitled "Groundhog Day" is utterly real. The endless recycling of policy pronouncements by governments, the total lack of memory – which means learning nothing from past successes or failures – and the critical point that policies never grapple with the challenges of implementation – all these things are described clearly and well. At a time when the commonwealth-led COAG arrangements involve clear government commitments to relevant outcomes, it remains true that delivery, rather than good intentions, is the problem. These are matters for other essays, but there is a vast gap between how commonwealth and state policies on remote communities are conceived and written up, and how they are delivered on the ground. We are therefore likely to follow what Noel describes as a predictable cycle. There will be public revelation and consternation about failure, followed by a new policy review, a new policy framework and a new commitment – with Groundhog Day occurring every three to five years. Cast your mind back to the last COAG communiqué issued in Darwin along with the Productivity Commission's report on (the lack of) progress and the point is made. Noel's response then was, "Groundhog Day"; mine, "Words words words – I am so sick of words."

But the most powerful message of the essay is that if there is to be cultural survival, it has to be in a bicultural context. Survival under the old ways of transmitting culture is not possible because there is no mechanism in the old culture for dealing with the negative aspects of the settler culture, no way to control alcohol, no way to deal with the temptation to do nothing when welfare is available. A full Western education – education to understand and to be able to function in the post-Enlightenment world – is a necessity for Aboriginal survival. So is educating non-Indigenous students to value Indigenous culture – an aspect of reconciliation not dealt with in Noel's essay, but alluded to when he says that the achievement of socio-economic equality and biculturalism "will require a significant change of attitude in … the wider Australian public."

I came to the conclusion that education was the key through a more anecdotal and less analytical path than Noel. My final conversion to the belief that education is the critical factor – and by this I mean education in the dominant culture and in standard Australian English – came from observing the eastern goldfields of Western Australia. Seeing the degraded lives of fringe dwellers in Kalgoorlie, in from the Central Desert, seeing them on country in such different circumstances, made the point. It was captured by a senior man from the desert, who told me: "I worked in Kalgoorlie and have seen the way that our people coming into Kalgoorlie are fit to be nothing but fringe dwellers."

Having seen the lamentable lives and circumstances of so many of the people coming into centres such as Darwin (the long grassers), Alice Springs, Halls Creek and Kalgoorlie, many of whom have dignity born of solid commitment to country and culture when on their home ground, has led me to the conclusion that the old way *by itself* is no longer viable.

Some wonderful, strong Aboriginal people will deny this. But I think the evidence is irrefutable. What some of those people fear is that the sort of education Noel espouses will mean they cease to be Aboriginal. This very point was put to me in Alice Springs. In a way, that fear is correct – if being Aboriginal means being locked into a static cultural situation, required to be sufficient unto itself, yet without the old disciplines born of the necessity to survive by one's own efforts in a harsh environment. This fear underlines the relevance of the first eleven pages of the essay. It is necessary to re-imagine what it is to be Aboriginal in a world of store food, Toyotas, new media, gambling, drugs and so on. The numerous Aboriginal people I know who are bicultural are living examples of the possibility that one can be Aboriginal and confident in the dominant society. That possibility is not clear to people whose self-definition is as outsiders.

This brings to mind Peter Sutton's recent book *The Politics of Suffering* and the intersection of his and Noel's perspectives on culture. Valuing and nurturing culture in this way stimulates it to develop and survive in new circumstances. Perhaps this gives us somewhere to go with Peter's analysis of the destructive role of dislocated, devalued culture in remote communities today.

I was greatly reassured by Noel's references to reconciliation and its relevance to his central themes of education and culture. My sense is that Noel's essay and Peter's book both argue a case for reconciliation that is entirely consistent with our own case at Reconciliation Australia. They challenge the simplification of reconciliation to the "close the gap" mantra, explaining there is more to it than that, although improving the material circumstances of Aboriginal people is undoubtedly an essential goal.

As Noel puts it, the recognition that education (and all the gaps that are linked to it) is central to reconciliation is entirely justified, but so too is "the question of Aboriginal people's place within the Australian sovereign state." As Reconciliation Australia understands it, there's a gap that needs to be closed between us as fellow Australians. Building relationships that allow us to work together to improve Aboriginal people's life chances needs to happen on many levels, from the national level Noel describes to the personal level to which Peter Sutton gives priority.

Noel's discussion of how to teach Aboriginal children canvasses the conflicting conservative and leftist educational views. To me, Noel's case for educating disadvantaged children by using conservative approaches to pedagogy is convincing because it is in accord with my own life and experience and that of my wider family. It is consistent with my observation of Aboriginal people educated conservatively (that is, they are numerate and literate and speak good English) now and in the past who have been able to live the lives they wish to lead. They are confident in two cultures and education has been the key to this.

We all see life through the prism of our own experience. Growing up in a public-housing area in Perth, I saw class and occupational differences. My teacher parents said they could leave us nothing, but their legacy would be a good education. Because my mother was Catholic and my non-Catholic father had been educated in Catholic schools by his Baptist mother, we all went to Catholic schools. I was acutely aware that they scrimped in order to pay our modest school fees. The parish school I attended was staffed by unpaid nuns – Brown Josephs – and those who could not pay did not. I was also aware from an early age that the Catholic schools were an exercise in lifting working-class kids into the middle class. It has been a successful exercise.

All of my many siblings and now their children have followed the path of education, enabling full involvement and engagement in Australian life. Whether it was business, law, medicine, politics, education, whatever we have aspired to be has been possible. In exactly the same way, I see Aboriginal people flourishing when they get a real educational opportunity. This goes beyond casual observation. Since 1997 a small private foundation I helped establish has worked with parents, schools and education authorities, mainly supported by the mining industry, to assist promising Aboriginal students to finish school in their own communities. The life possibilities for those who finish school are quite different from others in their cohort. They do not appear to be casting aside their Aboriginality in the process. Noel is right on the money in this regard. Truly equal education, a high standard of achievement in basic competencies, enables the disadvantaged, be they black, white or brindle, to take on the world on its terms. As Noel has pointed out, in this essay and elsewhere, high educational standards have not been destructive of Jewish identity.

Educationalists should feel some greater responsibility on reading this essay, but even more they should feel shame that, generations ago, Aboriginal people were getting a better education in literacy, numeracy and English from missionaries than many Aboriginal children are receiving today. When old men tell me that their children are "no good," I know it is not the children who have failed to learn; it is the teachers who have failed to teach.

It is a pity that Noel feels the need to challenge Chris Sarra and his approach to black pride as an educational tool. As a non-professional observer, I see much in common between Chris's approach and the No Excuses approach guiding Cape York educational reform. "Our culture is our strength" (Cape York) and "strong and smart" (Sarra) have much in common.

There may be something of an internal inconsistency in Noel's argument here. Is he suggesting that there is "Class" (Western education) and "Culture" (education in traditional languages etc.) and never the twain should meet? Or that while achievement in the latter depends on achievement in the former, the reverse is not the case? My view is that they are interconnected, just as pride in one's Aboriginal identity is connected with pride in culture.

If Aboriginal students aren't encouraged to take and show pride in their culture as a motivation for success, how can we encourage governments and the wider community to take pride in it, value it and invest in its survival, as Noel rightly asserts we must?

Most importantly, both Pearson and Sarra expect children to learn the full standard curriculum. Noel is correct to identify the common ground but does not emphasise what I think is the real difference between their approaches, with his focus on the use of income management as a tool, as against Sarra's belief that carrots are better than sticks in achieving parental and student involvement.

Comment could run on forever. The real point is to read the essay in full and for authorities to demand of their schools that classrooms be places where Aboriginal children are equipped for bicultural survival in the dominant culture, an outcome that is in all Australians' best interests.

Fred Chaney

Jane Caro

A relationship counsellor once described guilt to me as an absolutely useless emotion. It is the emotion you have, she said, when you feel the need to reassure yourself that you are – despite appearances to the contrary – a good person. We tend to feel guilt when we know we have behaved badly but have absolutely no intention of changing our behaviour, so, instead, we feel bad about whatever we have done to shore up our self-image. If we have really behaved badly, the counsellor argued, shame is a much better response, because shame feels so awful (nauseatingly, humiliatingly awful) that it is a real motivator to change. We can live with guilt, it seems, but not with shame.

With this in mind, I absolutely take Noel Pearson's point about much middle-class lefty rhetoric about Aboriginal Australians. I accept that many of us feel guilty about Aboriginal Australians and the shameful statistics in just about every area you care to mention regarding their life chances as compared to the rest of us. I also accept that much of our mealy-mouthed rhetoric about his people has been indulgent, designed to make us feel better, to shore up our own self-image, rather than actually do something concrete and effective about changing both the opportunities and outcomes for Aboriginal Australians.

I also accept that so far the education system in Australia has failed to improve very much for very many Indigenous people. As Pearson rightly points out, racism has had a lot to do with this lack of real progress, as has much of the well-meaning but ultimately self-serving rhetoric of earnest academics, reformers and pundits. But they have not stymied progress towards educational equality on their own.

According to Professor Barry McGaw, Australia has high-quality but relatively low-equity schooling compared with other high-quality countries. The troublesome "long tail" of under-achievement that dogs our every attempt to improve school performance keeps reminding us of this. Of course, there is no need to remind Noel Pearson that many Aboriginal school students can be found in that long tail. What is really tragic, however, is that, despite protestations to the contrary, Australia appears to be determinedly lengthening that tail, driving our most advantaged and most disadvantaged students even farther apart. We are doing this by developing a two-tiered education system comprising a well-resourced, partly publicly funded, fee-charging private-school sector for the better-off or the talented, and an ever less well-resourced, publicly funded sector for the rest.

The results of this thirty-year trend have been devastating for educational equality and for disadvantaged students of all kinds, including Aboriginal kids. In 1996, according to researcher Barbara Preston, there were thirteen students from low-income families to every ten students from high-income families in the playgrounds of our public high schools. By 2006, that had risen to sixteen low-income students to every ten high-income students. To put that another way, 26 per cent of students in independent schools are from high-income households, compared to 16 per cent at Catholic schools and a dwindling (and terrifying) 8 per cent at government schools.

Pearson hardly mentions public and private schooling in his essay except to make the following point: "If I have learned anything about public education, it is that it is thoroughly class-sensitive in its provisioning. What it provides to middle-class kids at Edge Hill in Cairns is palpably different to what it provides at Cairns West." He is, of course, right to the extent that public schools still reflect the community they serve. (Though, if Preston's figures are correct, then almost all public schools now enrol the poorest children in their area, even if their poverty is only relative.) But the relative inequality of public schools is no reason for governments and policy-makers to throw up their hands in despair and actively encourage the exit of the middle class from public education altogether. In wealthy metropolitan areas, Sydney's eastern suburbs for example, this separation of wealthier citizens from public education has reached extremes. There are only three public high schools left in Sydney's prosperous east, and two of them are single-sex. It is seriously worrying when not just the school but the school systems our children attend are predicated on the economic background or class aspirations of their parents. The only schools that are open to all are rapidly losing their middle-class families.

This matters because our most advantaged, influential and articulate citizens have less and less personally invested in the fortunes of the schooling system that educates more and more of our poorest and neediest children, including 88 per cent of Aboriginal children. Their energies, loyalties and abilities go into private education instead. It also matters because of the inevitable message it sends kids in public schools, no matter what colour their skin is. The message they receive is that they are less valuable, less desirable and less will be expected of them. Plucking a few fortunate kids from their local schools and exposing them to the heady world of the wealthy may help those lucky individuals, but it does nothing to help educational equality in this country and probably actively harms it.

This wholesale flight by better-off families from our public-education system is explained as the consequence of parental choice. Some blame what they see as "failing" public schools for driving those parents who can, to jump ship; others blame the compounding effect over decades of deliberate government policy, ideologically driven funding and an increasingly anxious population of middle-class parents with fewer children and much more money to spend on them. One thing over which there can be no dispute, however, is that parental choice is why some teachers and principals are starting to talk about an emerging "de facto apartheid" in our schooling system. In a recent survey, public-school principals expressed their concern about an increasing concentration of Indigenous kids in public schools and a corresponding flight of white kids to other schools, especially in rural areas.

Parental choice in some parts of Australia seems to mean choosing not to have your kid sit next to a black kid. In some parts of our major cities, it means choosing not to have your kid sit next to a kid in a hijab. Few admit to this as being part of the motivation behind their choice, although some of the less sophisticated are prepared to claim that private schools educate – and I quote – "a nicer class of kiddy." Most will make solemn – if ignorant – claims about private schools having better teachers and a better curriculum, even though all teachers are trained in the same unis in the same pedagogy that Pearson criticises so vigorously in his essay, and the curriculum is the same across public and private schools in all states of Australia. Some will admit to seeking better discipline, which I believe basically means that parents know naughty kids are more easily excluded from private schools than public ones.

Parental choice is applauded most by those who are considered to be on the right of the political divide, but make no mistake: middle-class lefties (while feeling suitably guilty about choosing a private school) also take full advantage of it.

However, I want to avoid (as much as I can) the terms "Left" and "Right" in my response to Pearson's essay. I believe the attempt to transplant the economic and ideological ideas that have formed our sense of the Left and Right wings of politics carries much of the responsibility for our growing educational inequality.

The market-driven ideas of capital and labour, and of the individual versus the collective, have caused much of the damage. Those who believe that competition and a free market can solve every conceivable problem are blind to the damage market forces are doing to the educational opportunities of our most disadvantaged children, and those who believe the interests of the collective should always triumph over those of the individual are blind to the hopes and fears of real, living, breathing human parents.

The British philosopher Stephen Law in his book *The War for Children's Minds* redraws the battlelines by demonstrating that rather than Left or Right, the real battle in education is between the authoritarians and the liberals.

What is fascinating about his redefinition is that it reveals how selectively both sides of the educational divide apply their particular philosophies. After all, parental choice looks very much like a liberal value – every individual parent should have the right to choose the best way to educate their children (if they can afford it, of course). Conversely, the pleas of those of us horrified by the demise of public education are often decried as authoritarian – wanting to force every family into the same, monolithic state-controlled mould. Yet, when it comes to what goes on in the classroom, each side neatly flips on its head. The pundits who are vociferous in their defence of parental choice often applaud an authoritarian pedagogy, while defenders of public education are often much more comfortable with a more liberal approach.

Pearson's essay, it seems to me – while he never uses the term – is about the effectiveness of an authoritarian approach to pedagogy, particularly for disadvantaged children and particularly for Aboriginal children. Indeed, the very names of the programs he extols indicate as much: "No Excuses," "Direct Instruction," "Prescriptive Teaching," even "Knowledge Is Power." As I am neither an Indigenous Australian nor an educator, I bow to his greater knowledge and understanding of what works inside a classroom for children who have been born and brought up in vastly different circumstances from my own. I remain bewildered, however, by his vociferous support for the phonics side of what I see as a phoney war between phonics and whole-language approaches to teaching children to read. It has never seemed to me that the phonics and whole-language approaches are mutually exclusive and I believe that most sensible classroom teachers agree with me. They read children stories (whole language), stick the names of things around the classroom (whole language) and help beginning readers to sound out the words (phonics). Surely we should ban neither and encourage both. Why must it be the carrot or the stick – why not a little of both, judiciously and appropriately applied?

Nevertheless, I am in awe of Pearson's dedication and determination to change the educational outcomes for the Indigenous children of Cape York. More strength to his arms, if the levers he pulls bring about favourable results.

What concerns me still, however, is the long-term future of educational equality in Australia. While a more authoritarian approach to pedagogy may help in some classrooms, the increasing socio-economic educational apartheid in our playgrounds cannot bode well. The elephant in the room in Australia's education system is that we have one group of publicly funded schools with all the rights (the right to choose who they will or won't educate, the right to choose where they will build schools, the right to charge whatever fees they deem appropriate, the right to expel the troublesome or the low-achieving) and another group of publicly funded schools with all the responsibilities – particularly when it comes to educating all Australian children, whoever they are, wherever they live, no matter what difficulties they bring through the school gate. And as long as that's how we design our education provision, we will never have any hope of achieving improvements in our long-term educational equality.

My radical hope is a curiously old-fashioned one. I hope that one day all our children, regardless of who their parents are, will have access to well-funded, inclusive schools. That the educational resources available to children in our most socially disadvantaged areas will be as good as, if not better than, those available to children who live in wealthier areas. I hope that our children will go to school and not just learn the curriculum but also that there are as many ways to live a good life as there are people living lives. But, most of all, I hope that the schools that are open to all children and that do not charge fees are regarded as the best, not just in the country, but in the world.

And I will feel not guilt but shame until they are.

Jane Caro

Andrew Leigh

In an international survey, a random sample of Australians and Americans were asked which factors were important to getting ahead in life. On most questions, the two groups concurred. But asked about education, nine out of ten Americans rated it "essential" or "very important," compared with just seven out of ten Australians. Subsequent research by the Australian National University's Youth in Focus team suggests that Australian income-support recipients are even less likely to believe that education matters.

Perhaps it should not be surprising that education is regarded as less important in the Lucky Country. By the 1940s, the typical American student had finished Year 12. It was not until the mid-1980s that the same could be said of young Australians. Today, about one in four Australian students still fails to complete high school. When US politicians speak to schoolchildren in low-income areas, they deliver the same message that they give their own children: study hard, finish school and go on to university if you can. When Australian politicians deliver speeches to young people in working-class neighbourhoods, they are much less likely to stress the value of formal education.

In this context, Noel Pearson's call for education to be at the core of Indigenous policy is refreshingly direct. It is not merely about increasing the quantity of education that Indigenous people receive, but also about raising the quality of that education. It asks more of government (particularly through raising teacher quality) but also of parents and students (in Pearson's words, "Aboriginal Australians must become a serious people").

Does school quality really matter? One of the strongest pieces of evidence on this point is that the black–white test-score gap widens over the lifecycle. According to the work that I have done with my colleague Xiaodong Gong, the typical Indigenous child starts school one year behind their non-Indigenous classmates. By the time they finish primary school, Indigenous children are two years behind. Paradoxically, I think this is good news for reformers, since schools are more amenable to policy intervention than families. Half the test-score gap can be closed simply by ensuring that Indigenous children learn at the same rate as non-Indigenous children while they are at school.

Pearson's essay touches on many of the critical issues for improving schools, not just in Indigenous communities but across the nation. He recollects a "hugely beneficial" fifth-grade teacher who had a major educational impact, yet whose name he can no longer recall. This emphasises that when it comes to effectiveness in the classroom, we should beware of formulas for successful teaching. Pearson also points out that instructional approaches and teacher quality are intimately related: the more talented the teacher, the more freedom the curriculum can allow them. He might have noted that the same is true of remuneration and dismissal: the case for merit pay would be weaker if it was easier to remove under-performing teachers.

Teaching disadvantaged children is perhaps the most important job in Australia. Yet we lack the innovative policies that would help to ensure that the most talented teachers are drawn to the most disadvantaged schools. The same reluctance characterises interventions to boost participation and performance. Where new policies have been trialled, it is generally in an ad hoc manner, leaving others uncertain about the efficacy of particular policies.

Recognising this, Pearson writes about the need for education policy-makers to rely more upon data and less on ideology. Discussing teaching methods, he cites the willingness of researchers to ignore Siegfried Engelmann's Direct Instruction approach, despite many rigorous studies backing it up. Pearson is right to point out the travesty of ignoring good evidence. But in most cases, we simply do not have high-quality evidence about what works.

To build the evidence base, it will be necessary for policy-makers to run the kinds of scientifically rigorous experiments that are commonplace in the medical literature. With a randomised experiment, you can be confident that differences between the treatment and control groups are truly causal. Without randomisation, we are usually left unsure whether changes in the treatment population are due to the policy or would have occurred anyway.

Randomised experiments would be a radical step in Indigenous policy. Some will contend that it is unethical to decide which individual gets a treatment based on the toss of a coin. Others will argue that local knowledge should determine which policies are implemented. Under this view, self-determination precludes randomised evaluation.

Yet randomised policy trials are simply the logical extension of Pearson's call for evidence over ideology. If the principles of the Enlightenment are to guide Indigenous education policies (as he advocates), then we need to begin putting some of our theories to the test. And the most rigorous test around is the randomised policy trial.

Of course, we already do this in Indigenous health policy. When it comes to assessing the effectiveness of a diabetes drug for Indigenous Australians, scientists and politicians would agree that it should be evaluated using a randomised control group. By tossing a coin, we ensure that the treatment group (for whom the coin came up heads) are as similar as possible to the control group (for whom the coin came up tails). And while we might conduct some focus groups on the side, the ultimate test would be effectiveness: did the new drug do a better job of treating the disease?

In the same vein, we should be willing to run experiments in Indigenous education: judging reforms on results, not just theory. Are we better off spending money on smaller classes or higher teacher salaries? Could we boost attendance by paying all Indigenous children $20 a week to show up to school? Do Indigenous children learn better from Indigenous teachers? Do children benefit more from longer school years or longer school days? Do nutrition programs have an educational pay-off? Does Direct Instruction raise both test scores and self-esteem for Indigenous Australian students? Could merit pay improve student learning, or would it just sow divisiveness in the staffroom? So far as I am aware, we have no rigorous randomised evidence from Australia on any of these interventions.

In international development, the large-scale adoption of randomised trials has been driven by the recognition that despite $2.5 trillion of foreign aid over the past half-century, many developing nations remain desperately poor. In the words of William Easterly, "planners" (with grand visions about how to end poverty) now need to be replaced by "searchers" (who rigorously test small-scale interventions). In Indigenous policy, most sensible policy-makers quietly agree that many of our policies are ineffective. Yet the policy debates are still dominated by planners, with their overarching theories. The evidence base remains paper-thin.

One of the things randomised trials have taught us is that impressive-sounding programs can flop. To take just one example, its boosters often argue that Neighbourhood Watch reduces crime. Going on theory alone, it is easy to tell compelling stories about how the program *should* be effective. Indeed, low-quality evaluations (using matched control groups, say) suggest that the program works. Yet randomised trials almost invariably find that Neighbourhood Watch does nothing to cut crime. Raise the evidence bar and the answer changes.

A move from ideology to empirics (from planning to searching, in Easterly's language) would require a good deal more modesty from policy-makers. Rather than judging programs based on case studies and theory, we could use the same rigour that we apply to new pharmaceuticals. Despite ideological battles over particular Indigenous policies, there is broad agreement over the "Closing the Gaps" targets. So why not rigorously assess each new Indigenous intervention according to whether or not it can be proven to help close one or more of the gaps?

The urgency of the problem should not be an excuse for lowering the evidence bar. The federal government would never have funded this year's nationwide rollout of swine-flu vaccine without seeing the results of randomised clinical trials. Yet the 2007 intervention was implemented across the Northern Territory with zero randomised evidence. If we want to know the causal impact of banning pornography, quarantining welfare or scrapping CDEP, a handful of randomised trials would tell us more than overblown rhetoric and angry accusations ever could.

Once we raise the evidence bar in Indigenous education, we may look back and wonder how we ever settled for less. In the United States, a strong advocate of randomised trials in education is Roland Fryer, the youngest African-American ever to become a full professor at Harvard. In an interview last year, he told the New York Times: "If the doctor said to you, 'You have a cold; here are three pills my buddy in Charlotte uses and he says they work,' you would run out and find another doctor. Somehow, in education, that approach is OK."

Fryer is currently running a series of randomised experiments across Chicago, New York and Washington D.C., evaluating interventions such as high-quality charter schools and paying students who receive good grades. The essence of his approach is humility in the face of data. As he puts it: "We will have the willingness to try new things and be wrong – the type of humbleness to say, 'I have no idea whether this will work, but I'm going to try.'"

There are many proposals to love in Pearson's eloquent essay. But can we meld his careful ideas and deep experience with Fryer's scientific rigour? Or, to put it another way, Pearson may well be right, but is he willing to be wrong?

Andrew Leigh

Noel Pearson

I have been working with colleagues and community leaders on a proposal to develop No Excuses schools in remote communities in Cape York Peninsula. Our proposition to the commonwealth and Queensland governments is to establish a Cape York Aboriginal Australian Academy, a specialist kindergarten to Year 7 remote-schools provider which will have legislative delegation within the Queensland public school system to provide education where Indigenous parent communities support this alternative. Our proposed reform model will strengthen public education. While there are many features that differ from existing provisioning, most of these have a strong resonance with prevalent thinking about educational reform.

If any point is fundamental to our academy proposal, it is its governance. We are seeking the necessary delegation of autonomy to enable an independent board to provide the direction and support to the educators in the communities whom we will rely upon to deliver our vision. We want to replace governance by the system with governance by a group of people who see their role as enabling and assisting the educators to create not just a school or a group of schools, but a high-quality and lasting institution. Institutions take time to build, but when they have been established they have momentum and longevity that outlast the changing of personnel. Institutions have those intangible things – values, culture, traditions, expectations, pride, attachment and so on – which can make success self-perpetuating and sustainable over time.

The problem with small schools generally, and with remote communities in particular, is that the fast turnover of teaching personnel (the three-year average in Cape York is about as good as we can expect) and of school leadership – and the absence of any formal leadership engagement of Aboriginal people – means that it is impossible to develop an institution that embeds and sustains a culture of high expectations and no excuses. There have been many times when schools served by great teachers or great school leaders have shown great promise – but you're back to square one when the next leader comes along.

As well as remoteness, the small scale of these schools makes the development of a high-quality institution almost impossible because of the constant flux. The answer is to create networks of grouped schools where an institutional identity can capture both a local and a wider network identity – the creation of state colleges in Weipa in Cape York Peninsula and Thursday Island in Torres Strait has gone a long way towards this.

I believe that the academy we have proposed will only work if I and other like-minded people who are passionate and competent are able to mandate the ethos and culture of the kind of institution that is needed: this is what is so hard to achieve with traditional public schooling, particularly at the scale with which we are dealing. I am not saying that a No Excuses, Best of Both Worlds philosophy is the only possible kind of school ethos and approach that can work. Educators with different views, such as Chris Sarra, should also be given the autonomy to chart Indigenous education-reform programs within the public education system.

The intended structure of the academy was only briefly and indirectly described in my *Quarterly Essay*. The public presentation of our plan, to which the correspondents did not have access, has clarified some issues that are of concern to them. For example, we do not believe we can reform remote education as an "autonomous field" in isolation from "interrelated areas" such as health, housing and so on, as Christine Nicholls suspected was the case. Reform of education supply is very much an integral part of a comprehensive development agenda.

However, most of the comments in the rich harvest of correspondence have stimulated me to grapple further with fundamental questions. The correspondents raised issues that fall into two broad categories. First, Indigenous educational failure may be seen as our most extreme example of social disadvantage, without any particular regard paid to the larger issue of Indigenous Australians' place in our nation. Questions of culture and self-determination may be relevant to this kind of discussion, but fundamentally Aboriginal reconciliation is defined as closing the social and economic gap. The objective of policy is not to institute further recognition of the special status of Indigenous Australians, and no assumption is made that such recognition is conducive to educational advancement. The question is simply what sets Indigenous children on a life trajectory of successful schooling, tertiary study and prosperity.

Second, education may be viewed from the point of view of cultural self-determination and preservation of Indigenous Australian culture.

Most correspondents apply both perspectives. The only correspondent who discusses my essay purely from the former angle is Andrew Leigh. He correctly observes that "teaching disadvantaged children is perhaps the most important job in Australia" and he appears to view Indigenous education solely as an issue of removing educational disadvantage. The question Leigh implicitly asks is, "How do we find out which policies will lift Indigenous academic achievement to mainstream standards?" He reads my suggestion that Aboriginal Australians have a serious discussion about what it might mean to be "a serious people" as an exhortation to Aboriginal parents to become engaged in their children's education and to Aboriginal students to work harder – which is correct, but not the whole point I tried to make.

Nonetheless, Leigh's response is important because he insists that "the urgency of the problem should not be an excuse for lowering the evidence bar." The only evidence that will ultimately be of any value, Leigh argues, is randomised trials. Leigh is probably Australia's most consistent advocate of rigorous randomised trials as the sole meaningful basis for evidence-based policy. Because of the absence of systematic formulation and trialling of conceivable policies, we "do not have high-quality evidence about what works," and the range of policies that have been tried is limited.

Leigh perceptively observes that "self-determination precludes randomised evaluation." The establishment of our academy proposal will depend on an active choice by local parent communities and elected leaders.

The comments by Peter Shergold (and Jane Caro's plea for educational equality in Australia) are likewise mainly concerned with bridging "the appalling chasm of disadvantage." Shergold challenges my assertion that bureaucracies have no memory. Many individual public servants indeed remember the lack of substance behind so much vainglorious political rhetoric, Shergold writes. But he goes on to concede that the experience of public servants "too often feeds hard-nosed cynicism."

I did not mean to imply that all public servants with first-hand experience suffer from amnesia when I asserted that governments and bureaucracies have no memory – I said that true memory entails moral responsibility, which is the opposite of cynicism.

Christine Nicholls, who lived and worked for many years as an educator and school principal in a remote community where an Aboriginal language is still the first language, is naturally more engaged in her discussion of the preservation of Australia's Aboriginal cultures as a goal in its own right – an indispensable element of reconciliation. Nicholls writes that my "aspiration to hold on to

Aboriginal knowledge and cultural practices, languages and traditions, some of which are experiencing severe strain, is of the utmost importance" and supports my "insistence that governments, as well as individuals, have critically important responsibilities in this respect." Nicholls notes that Australia's remaining Aboriginal languages are in urgent need of legislative protection.

However, Nicholls' advocacy for new policies for the survival of Australia's national minorities is no more passionate than could be expected from an educator and academic with her experience and research interests. The most important reaction to my essay has come from the most culturally conservative quarters.

Tony Abbott concludes that the importance of a "standard academic education" and "the need for Aboriginal people to be able to participate in the broader economy on their merits" are not the main points of my essay. "Effective participation in wider society," Abbott writes, "is more a by-product of the education that [Pearson] wants for young Aborigines; it's not the main objective."

That is perhaps overstating it. Man cannot live by bread alone, but he does need bread, and in the modern world the broader economy is where he'll earn it. But Abbott recognises that, even though my texts (including my *Quarterly Essay*) are often perceived to mainly challenge the Left, the bigger challenge may well be reserved for the Right.

The political Right will probably be divided on this challenge. Those on the culturally shallow Right, whose conservatism does not extend far beyond simple advocacy for economic liberalism, will not instinctively grasp, as Abbott does, that the challenge is "to accept that biculturalism, at least for Aboriginal people, is a worthy object of Australian government policy and is worth paying for."

Christopher Pearson responded to my *Quarterly Essay* in the *Weekend Australian* on 31 October 2009 with words similar to Abbott's:

> Noel Pearson ... invokes the example of Jews and their remarkable successes in the fields of both mainstream academic instruction and maintenance of a distinctive culture. He thinks that without the active support of state and private schools, combined with higher overall standards and sustained formal instruction in Aboriginal languages and traditions, indigenous high cultures will vanish.
>
> If there were one priority in national cultural policy on which most of us could wholeheartedly agree, surely this is it ... If we want there to be a rising generation fluent in Pitjantjatjara and the other main endangered language groups – apart from geriatrics and

European linguists – we must encourage and reward them and the people who train them.

Creole or children's versions of Aboriginal languages are no more suitable to ceremony or the recitation of Dreaming stories than are colloquial English or playground slang to the articulation of the meta-narratives of the West. Whether Aboriginal religions can be re-invigorated, as opposed to indigenous cultures in a more general sense, remains to be seen. But turning a blind eye to an existing education system that deprives indigenous kids of an adequate grounding in either the basics of ordinary education or their own cultures is philistinism on a grand scale.

Christopher Pearson's article convinces me that Tony Abbott's principled response to my essay is not necessarily unrepresentative of conservative Australian thinking and a mere product of Abbott's close association with Cape York reform projects and his friendship with my colleagues and myself (or, for that matter, of his friendship with Christopher Pearson). A common chord is struck with conservatives.

The explanation is, of course, that serious conservatives such as Abbott and Pearson understand the existential importance of "meta-narratives" and of languages, literatures and spiritual traditions for their own sake in a way that well-intentioned but culturally modernist supporters of Aboriginal people do not, be they from the right-of-centre, left-liberal or progressive bands of the political spectrum.

Christopher Pearson and Tony Abbott intuitively understand that Aboriginal Australians' languages and traditions are at the spiritual centre of our nation and that they are not only for Aboriginal Australians. Furthermore, they realise that the cathedral is on fire.

Abbott suspects that I underestimate the magnitude of the task of maintaining, revitalising and reviving Australia's own culture. I do not. On the contrary, I suspect that the public does not understand the grave problems of Aboriginal languages and traditions as they are now, including those languages and traditions that are believed to be relatively intact. There needs to be a rapid development of the material and institutional infrastructure supporting our languages and cultures. The number of non-Indigenous Australians competent in our languages and cultures needs to increase by several orders of magnitude within the next few years. What needs to be done needs to be the subject of a separate discussion.

In my Judith Wright Lecture in 2004, I concluded that:

> The political truism that only Nixon could go to China is pertinent here. Only a highly conservative leader, one who enjoys the confidence of the most conservative sections of the national community – those in rural and regional Australia – will be able to lead the country to an appropriate resolution of these issues. It will take a prime minister in the mould of Tony Abbott to lead the nation to settle the "unfinished business" between settler Australians and the other people who are members of this nation: the Indigenous people.

In that speech I was mainly (but, of course, not exclusively) referring to a national agreement that would settle land issues, economic and social issues and constitutional recognition of Indigenous Australians. The names might change, but the political analysis stands.

I regret that I cannot respond to all issues raised by the correspondents. Fred Chaney's deeply personal text demonstrates that a readiness to participate in the maintenance and development of Australia's cultures is perhaps more widespread than I thought.

Noel Pearson

Tony Abbott is the shadow minister for Families, Community Services and Indigenous Affairs and serves on the House of Representatives standing committee for Aboriginal and Torres Strait Islander Affairs.

Jane Caro is the co-author, with Chris Bonnor, of *The Stupid Country: How Australia Is Dismantling Public Education* (2007).

Fred Chaney is a former minister for Aboriginal Affairs and a research fellow in Aboriginal affairs, policy and administration at the University of Western Australia. He was a member of the National Native Title Tribunal and is currently a director of Reconciliation Australia.

Andrew Leigh is a professor in the Research School of Economics at the Australian National University. His research is on the economics of education, labour economics and public finance.

Mungo MacCallum is one of Australia's most influential political journalists. Over a career spanning more than four decades, he has worked for most of Australia's leading newspapers and magazines and been a journalist and broadcaster for the ABC and SBS. His books include *Mungo: The Man Who Laughs, How To Be a Megalomaniac* and *Poll Dancing: The Story of the 2007 Election*.

Christine Nicholls is a senior lecturer in Australian studies at Flinders University. She is a former principal of Lajamanu School in Yuendumu.

Noel Pearson is a lawyer and activist, and the director of the Cape York Institute for Policy and Leadership. He is the author of *Up from the Mission* (2009).

Chris Sarra is the director of the Queensland government's Institute for Aboriginal and Torres Strait Islander Leadership. He was previously principal of the Cherbourg State School.

Peter Shergold was secretary of the Department of the Prime Minister and Cabinet from 2003 to 2008. He is a former head of the Aboriginal and Torres Strait Islander Commission and today heads the Centre for Social Impact at the University of New South Wales.

Peter Sutton is an anthropologist at the University of Adelaide and the South Australian Museum. His most recent book is The Politics of Suffering: Indigenous Australia and the End of the Liberal Consensus (2009).

www.ingramcontent.com/pod-product-compliance
Lightning Source LLC
Chambersburg PA
CBHW080206300326

41934CB00038B/3385